Behold
Your
Life

Behold
Your
Life

A
Pilgrimage
Through
Your Memories

Macrina Wiederkehr

ave maria press

Notre Dame, Indiana

© 2000 by Macrina Wiederkehr
International Standard Book Number: 0-87793-931-4
Cover and text design by: Maurine Twait
Printed and bound in the United States of America.

Weiderkehr, Macrina.
    Behold your life: a pilgrimage through your memories / Macrina Weiderkehr.
        p. cm.
    Includes bibliographical references.
    ISBN 0-87793-931-4 (paperback)
        1. Memory — Religious aspects — Christianity — Prayer-books and devotions
    — English. I. Title

BV4597.565.W45 1999
248.4'6—dc21
                                                                    99-048226

For the faith community

of St. Mary's Church

in Altus, Arkansas

where I was baptized and received

my early spiritual formation,

with special memory

of our founding pioneer families

whose brave hearts, deep faith, and dedication

inspire me to this day.

Appreciations

A heartfelt thank you to:

my growing community of retreatants
    for sharing with me the blessing of their lives;

Sisters Norbert Hoelting, Magdalen Stanton, Gabriel Brandt
    for their generous gift of time given in editing and
    proofreading;

Dolores Dietz, Joyce Rupp, Judith Weaver, Rebecca Wiederkehr,
    soul-sisters from whose wells I am often refreshed;

Bob Phillips,
    whose courageous struggle blesses me
    more than he will ever know;

Bob and Joyce Rogers
    for providing me with the sacred space
    needed for this book's completion;

Larry Neeb and James Adams of Creative Communications
    whose invitation to write one of their seasonal devotionals
    became the seed for this new book;

And finally, a special blessing for the folks at Ave Maria Press,
    especially Robert Hamma, my coach and editor.
I am grateful for your partnership
    in the birthing of *Behold Your Life.*

Contents

A Bit of History

This book had its beginnings with Creative Communications as their 1988 lenten devotional. In trying to decide upon a topic, I felt drawn to write something on memories and healing. Many times I had been led through a "healing of memories" prayer service, yet I often seemed to be left with a heavy feeling that came, I believe, from trying to cram my entire life into a few hours. I thought, "How good it would be to lead people through a journey of healing that would not be rushed." The results of my thoughts and efforts turned out to be a thirty-two page booklet in the form of a lenten retreat. It was entitled *Embracing Your Memories: A Journey of Healing for Lent.*

One of the unique things about this lenten *healing-of-memories* booklet is that it guided readers on a journey in which they focused not only on their painful memories, but also on their joyful memories. The Sundays of Lent were used to pray with the joyful memories, stressing that our joyful memories can actually be a means of healing some of the painful memories.

This devotional was a great success. However, since Creative Communications' intent was to have it as part of their 1988 lenten offering, it had a life span of only about three years. Although *Embracing Your Memories* is no longer in print, we continue to get many requests for it. I decided to revise it and bring it out again, not just as a lenten retreat but as a forty-day retreat for any season of your life.

When I began writing *Gold in Your Memories: Sacred Moments, Glimpses of God,* I thought that I was writing the revision of *Embracing Your Memories;* however, I soon discovered that books have a mind of their own and *Gold in Your Memories* took off in a different direction than originally planned. I allowed it to go the path of its choice. I am learning to listen to books and let them have their way.

Obviously, the book you are now holding, *Behold Your Life,* is the revised edition of *Embracing Your Memories.* It finally gave me its blessing and wants you to enjoy its new growth.

Hot Springs Village, Arkansas
June 20, 1999

Preparation *for* Your Journey

As one's trust in the hidden goodness of life becomes stronger,
it will be possible to bless more and
more of life's ambiguities.

—Demetrius Dumm

Pilgrimages have been an important part of religious history throughout the ages. A pilgrimage is a ritual journey with a hallowed purpose. Every step along the way has meaning. The pilgrim knows that the journey will be difficult and that life-giving challenges will emerge. A pilgrimage is not a vacation; it is a transformational journey during which significant change takes place. New insights are given. Deeper understanding is attained. New and old places in the heart are visited. Blessings are received. Healing takes place. On return from the pilgrimage, life is seen with different eyes. Nothing will ever be quite the same again.

I offer you this book as a forty-day retreat—a pilgrimage for your soul. It will be a ritual journey to the sacred site of your life's hidden goodness. In walking through these meditations you will be asked to embrace and bless life's ambiguities. The ambiguities of life often come in the shape of a cross. Many pilgrims have traveled the Via Dolorosa—the way of the cross! I have always been tempted to turn away from the cross, for it speaks of contradictions and paradoxes in my life. It speaks of things I do not understand while I long for clarity; yet the way of the pilgrim is never crystal clear. The cross is the banner carried by many pilgrims. The other side of the cross points toward resurrection. With that in mind, embracing the cross can lead to life.

The cross you are to embrace on this prayerful journey is your life, with all its pains and joys. I am suggesting that you take up your life and walk consciously and gratefully through these forty days. The Hebrew people journeyed through the wilderness searching for the promised land for forty days. Jesus fasted for forty days. The church offers us a forty-day period of renewal each year: the season of Lent.

You are about to embark on a forty-day journey through your life. Each day you will be asked to embrace specific memories. I've chosen to focus on the *embracing* of your memories rather than a *healing* of your memories. Embracing implies a recognition and acceptance that must take place in order for the memory to be integrated into your life in such a way that

11

healing can take place. Thus, the goal is not so much healing as acceptance. The healing comes through the acceptance.

In her enlightening book *My Name Is Chellis & I'm in Recovery from Western Civilization,* Chellis Glendinning speaks about the potential for personal recovery from the traumas in our lives. She quotes her therapist as saying, "In my experience . . . and with hundreds of patients, I can tell you that your condition is not 99.99% healable. It is 100% healable."[1] For those of us who are using the path of memories to find our way back home this is, indeed, good news.

In order to experience healing it is imperative that we find the courage to look upon our wounds and integrate them into our lives. Sometimes we suffer from the decision to remain a victim. It is so easy, and at times feels so right, to spend our lives blaming. We can wallow in self-pity and choose to live embittered lives because of the wrongs done to us. That is certainly a choice we are free to make. But there is another way. In this other way we compassionately befriend our wounds. Only then can we embrace our lives and look at our wounds without judgement. Thus, we learn experientially that what we wallow in will make us sick, and what we embrace will restore us to health.[2]

Throughout the gospels the compassion of Jesus flows out like a river. In his ministry of healing we see Jesus restoring people to health and giving them hope. All he asks in return is that they take up their lives and go on with their living. They are to claim the healing and move on with life. Moreover, he often reminds them that their healing has taken place not only because of what he has done for them, but also because of their faith. "Your faith has healed you," Jesus says to the blind Bartimaeus (Mark 10:52).

Perhaps, then, as you ponder the areas in your life where healing is needed, you, too, can bring the ointment of faith to your wounds. You are a cohealer with Jesus. You say to God, "My life is in your hands," and indeed it is. At the same time, it is good to remember that your life is also in your hands. No matter what the trauma of your past might be, you have the choice to pick up your life and continue. The challenge is to find the joy and strength that live amid the scars of life. You have been given the grace to assist God in bringing about the spiritual and emotional health needed to live a rich and joyful life.

In Numbers 21:4-9 of the Hebrew scriptures we see the Israelites playing out the role of victim. The desert was harsh. They were hungry and thirsty for a better life and better food. Suddenly no part of this journey looked like the road to freedom. They were in a season of murmuring. Then something happened even more dreadful than their hunger. They were bitten by desert serpents. The story reads that Yahweh asked Moses to erect a symbol of the very thing that had bitten them—a serpent. He was to hold up the replica of that brazen serpent; all who looked upon it would recover. They were asked to look upon the very thing that had bitten them. They were to look upon that which had wounded them. Only then could they be healed.

Can you find here a parallel for your own life? This forty-day pilgrimage through the wilderness of your life may not always look like the road to freedom, but I'm asking you to do what the Hebrew people were asked to do: look upon that which has wounded you. This is necessary for your recovery. Chellis Glendinning suggests that once the barriers of amnesia and denial are broken, the process of healing can begin. Using a dynamic illustration from a client involved in healing work, she describes the process as "a deep-sea dive to a sunken ship to reclaim lost treasure."[3]

During this prayerful journey I am asking you to reclaim the lost treasures of your life in whatever way is necessary. This may mean a deep-sea dive down to what appears to be the sunken ship of your own life. Or, it may mean descending into the deep earth of yourself to search out buried blessings. Like the Hebrew people in the desert, you, too, have been bitten—not by serpents perhaps, but I suspect that each of you has a story to tell about the bite of life. The bitter sting of some of life's heartrending stories often keeps the blessings hidden from our eyes. And yet, just as you have been bitten, so too have you been blessed.

13

In the days that follow call back into your memory some of the things that have bitten and blessed you throughout your life. Look upon your wounds to see if you might find some hidden blessings, for as Patricia McCarthy reminds us in this wisdom statement, "To believe in the resurrection means that we cannot stop at our wounds."[4] Her wisdom echoes that of Demetrius Dumm, "As one's trust in the hidden goodness of life becomes stronger, it will be possible to bless more and more of life's ambiguities.[5] Spend some time meditating on these quotations. What is your personal experience of resurrection in the midst of ambiguity? When was the last time you discovered and began to trust some hidden goodness in your life?

We take up our lives and walk. With life in one hand and death in the other, we walk in faith and hope. The rhythms of life and death move through our being. Life blesses us and we are grateful. We hold life's gifts dear. There is much that we cherish. At the same time we taste death in its many wrenching forms of denial, rejection, and separation. Yet in the midst of all our death we eventually rise again. Out of the ashes of our lives new roots emerge, green shoots appear, resurrection takes place. The dying and rising of Jesus continues to unfold in our lives. It is a drama of life and death that has continued throughout the centuries: the dying and rising of Oscar Romero, Joan of Arc, Dorothy Day, Martin Luther King Jr., Mother Teresa, and you, dear reader, yes, YOU! At the altar of daily life this drama forever unfolds. The seed of life that cannot be obliterated shows its face again and again in countless ways. Death cannot crowd out meaning if our hearts remain open to the unceasing outpouring of life. In the Christian tradition we call this flow of life, death, life, death, life, the paschal mystery.

This pilgrimage through your life will be fueled by that mystery—a mystery so alluring that we are forever drawn forward—even when we're reluctant to go. It is the paschal journey with Jesus through the shadows of life and death. You are to take up your life and walk through these shadows. Along the way, here are some questions to ask yourself: Am I beginning this journey with an open heart? Do I truly want to know myself? Is there a part of me that has closed the door to life? Do I fear this journey in any way? Is there a wound in my life that I've never talked about with anyone? Whom might I ask, in some small way, to accompany me on this journey? Am I willing to go slow and not hurry through these meditations? What is it that keeps me going each day? What is my hope that won't go away? Am I able to see grace at my fingertips? Is there a door that needs to be opened so that I can experience life more fully? Am I willing to allow myself to be resurrected?

Imagine that you are standing before the door of whatever tomb you've sealed yourself into. Listen to the voice of a friend calling out to you,

> I called through your door,
> "The mystics are gathering
> in the street. Come out!"
>
> "Leave me alone.
> I'm sick."
>
> "I don't care if you're dead!
> Jesus is here, and he wants
> to resurrect somebody."[6]

Jesus always wants to resurrect us. Our task is to open the door or roll away the stone that prevents us from experiencing life to the fullest. "I came that they might have life and have it to the full" (John 10:10). That fullness is always available. Sometimes it's part of the hidden goodness that we suddenly find in the midst of our ambiguities. Or perhaps it's hidden in the buried blessings of our lives and we just need to engage ourselves in a little digging to find it. The fact that something isn't visible does not mean it isn't present. It may be very near—waiting to be discovered. So take up your life and walk into an even fuller, more abundant life.

Blessings on your journey!

A Few Suggestions for Your Retreat

This forty-day pilgrimage has been planned with the intent that you move through the experience one day at a time. It would probably be helpful for you if you could do your meditation at the same time each day and even in the same place, but this may not always be possible. Improvise as you need to fit your life situation. If you are able to take a block of time in the morning, you could carry the theme with you throughout the day and perhaps use the closing prayer again at your day's end. My hope is that these meditations will enable you to slow down, to look kindly upon your life, to experience gratitude, joy, and healing.

Two people who prayed with the original *Embracing Your Memories* told me they started with day one and just kept on going because they couldn't stop. I smile as I ask you to refrain from reading all forty meditations in one sitting. Just like your vitamins—one a day is recommended. If, for some reason, you miss a day, just continue the next day where you left off.

As you begin this retreat I suggest you create a banner, perhaps in the shape of a cross, that you hang in your place of prayer. Each day you might want to put a small symbol representing your theme for that day on your banner. Look upon it and be healed as the Hebrew people looked upon the replica of the serpent and were healed.

Some people find journaling helpful. You may wish to purchase a new journal. Use this journal as you pray with your memories each day. Fill it with drawings, poetry, haiku, prayers, stories, images, letters. Write or draw in your journal in whatever way the Spirit leads you. This is your book of life. It is a mosaic of your memories. Embrace them and accept healing.

Blessings
on Your Journey

As you begin this pilgrim journey
   may your heart be open to surprise.

With reverence, gratitude, and acceptance
   may you behold your life each day.

On every step along the way
   may hidden goodness come to meet you.

In meditating on your memories
   may courage be your companion.

As your life-stories rise up to greet you
   may you welcome them home with love.

On every step of your pilgrimage
   may you find new grace for living.

From unexpected places in your life
   may blessings rise up to anoint you.

As you walk the memory road
   may it become a path of transformation.

As you look upon your wounds
   may you know the joy of healing.

In claiming the beauty of your life
   may you recognize the One
   in whose image you are created.

In moving beyond the wounds
   may you be able to take up your life
   and go on with your living.

Blessings on your journey!

A Forty-Day Pilgrimage

There is nothing in your life
too terrible or too sad
that will not be your friend
when you find the right name to call it,
and calling it by its own name
hastening
it will come upright to your side.

—Laurens van der Post

Day 1

*Remember you are dust; and unto dust
you shall return.*

From the liturgy of Ash Wednesday

Read Genesis 2:4-8

> *One day while walking through a meadow, a momentary
> awareness caused me to pause with reverence. Every person
> who ever lived upon this earth is still here. Their bodies have
> returned to the earth. Their spirits, too, in some mysterious
> and incomprehensible manner, linger in the land. Heaven
> and earth touch.*
>
> *Inspired by that insight, the meadow began to take on
> a sacred nature. The dust of the earth! Holy! How easy it is
> for the sacredness of the earth to escape us. How easy it is to
> forget. Today will be a dusty day. You are to remember the
> earth from which you came. Look upon your humble begin-
> nings and remember. The word humble comes from humus
> meaning "earth." Remember the truth that you came from
> the earth and shall return to the earth.*
>
> *This is a day for embracing your beginnings. Your
> imagination will be a helpful tool for your prayer on this
> first day of retreat. Welcome the earth from which you came
> and to which you shall return. Let this day be an earthy day.
> If possible pray with your feet in the soil. If this is not work-
> able for you, your imagination will serve you just fine.
> Today then, at the beginning of your retreat, I want you to
> embrace your memories of the earth. Where are your sacred
> places on this earth? Revisit those places in your mind.*

Earth! When it's dry, it's dust. When it's moist, it's clay. In the
eye of my mind, I paint this scene: the Divine Artist breathing upon the earth. A glorious moment in time! Creatures more

blessed than angels are being kneaded out of the earth. Humanity is lifted out of clay. Saints are being formed from the dust of the earth. God's breath moistens the clay and the process begins. Life arrives. Hearts begin to beat. One day my heart will be among them.

How difficult it has been throughout the ages to keep this heart pure. The clay, moist! I look upon the clay fondly as I celebrate the memory of my earthy beginnings. How often this heart of clay has dried up! How often it has cried out from its desert places! How often the Creator has heard my cry and made my dusty heart moist again with a warm and sacred breath. How often God has used other people to breathe life back into me!

Today as I begin this forty-day journey, I gaze back into time. I am dreaming about those "in the beginning" times. I see the Divine Artist holding a handful of clay. As I behold this scene I behold my life and remember my humble beginnings. It is not just myself I am gazing upon. It is the dust of the whole human race made moist with the breath of God. All of my ancestors are there in the palm of God's hands. I go outside and stand upon the earth. I kneel upon the earth. With deep reverence I scoop up a handful of soil. I take a moment to be in communion with all my relatives formed from the dust of the earth. This is my family: the entire human race, the animals, the birds, the trees, the plants, and the flowers. We are relatives—intimately connected. This is holy ground!

O God from whose hands I have come, God of wisdom and creativity, on some days I cry out in dismay that I am dust. That dusty memory is painful. Today I forgive you for my humble beginnings. The truth that you are the Source of my life begins to settle into the soil of my soul. Nourished with that truth, I bless you. I bless you who first blessed me. I bless this dust that is destined for glory. I allow the memory of this holy dust to comfort me. Embracing my simple beginnings, I place a speck of dust upon the banner of my cross as I begin this journey. Amen.

Day 2

Before I formed you in the womb
you were contained in my being.
I have known and cherished you forever.

Read Jeremiah 1:4-9

> *On this second day of retreat, contemplate the intimacy of being known and loved before you were born. This day takes place before you were in the womb. It is a time of simply being held and cherished for all eternity in the mind and heart of God. Just as you have always lived in the mind of God, allow yourself to preexist in your own mind. This is your chance to totally accept your life. Do you want to BE? Where were you before you were conceived in the womb? Can you love yourself that far back?*

I move now from the common universal dust of the human race to the more intimate and personal dust of me as an individual.

To be known before I was conceived in the womb! Is this not a breathtaking intuition? Somewhere in the mind and heart of God I always existed—not in the form I live in now, but in some secret, obscure manner I was present even at the creation of the world. I am putting that truth on my banner today. I am writing it in my journal. I am listening to the truth that I was known even before I lived in my mother's womb.

I imagine that this is the day before my conception. So what do you do on the day before your conception? Who are you? What are you? Where are you?

In his delightful collection of Christmas stories, *Tracks in the Straw,* Ted Loder gives us a conversation between an angel and the unborn. The unborn is not even in the womb yet. It is somewhere out on a star waiting to be sent. The angel is preparing it for its journey, explaining to it how human beings are both beautiful and complicated, how they create and destroy, struggle and love, how they live for awhile on the earth and finally die. The unborn is a bit reluctant to go on this journey. Here is a little of the conversation between the angel and the unborn:

> **Angel:** . . . Sometimes when it's a little quiet, mothers and fathers listen to a baby's heartbeat before the baby is born.
> **Unborn:** They can do that?
> **Angel:** Oh, yes!
> **Unborn:** What does it sound like?
> **Angel:** It sounds like the heart of God. . . . Well, I think you're about ready to go. We've covered about everything.
> **Unborn:** Ready? I still have a million questions. Besides, I haven't even packed yet.
> **Angel:** You don't have to pack. You can't take anything with you. . . . Whatever you need to wear will be provided for you when you get there.
> **Unborn:** But I have to make an entrance, don't I? I have to have something to arrive in.
> **Angel:** No, you don't. . . .
> **Unborn:** (With agitation) You mean to tell me that to get born on earth, you not only have to forget everything you ever learned here, AND become small and helpless, AND risk being taken care of by human beings who are complicated and confused, AND who fight a lot about things, AND are afraid most of the time, AND get old and die and worry about it, but to top it all off, you have to start out being absolutely, positively, completely stark naked?
> HAS ANYONE SPOKEN TO GOD ABOUT THIS?
> NAKED IS THE LAST STRAW![7]

Yes, we come into this world naked and poor, empty, small and dependent. As I muse on all that I will have to go through in living my life, I am tempted to ask the question Robert Benson asks in his book *Between the Dreaming and the Coming*

True, "Why didn't God just keep us, instead of sending us here to wander through all of this stuff we call life?"[8]

I don't really know the answer to that question and on some days Benson's question becomes my own. And yet, when my head clears up and my far-seeing eyes return, I am glad God didn't keep me. I am pleased to have been sent.

Eternal Source of Life, I am ready to become more than I am. I am ready to be sent. I do not know the way, but if your love for the world includes my presence in it, I am willing to live there. I ask only that you prepare a place for me and that you accompany me on the journey. Be there when I arrive and be there when I depart. And be there in all the in-between times. As I move into this new and unexplored land, my life is in your hands. Send me and receive me. Be with me every day of my life. Amen.

Day 3

Long before the world began,
I was a spark of God's love.
I was already chosen in the heart of God
to be holy, to be dear.

Read Ephesians 1:4-6

> *This is going to be the day of your conception. If you know the place or the city where you were conceived it may be helpful to imagine it or even to return to the place. The important aspect of this day is that it is a day for you to begin residing in your mother's womb. This day you are sent. This is a day to say "yes" to life. Your acceptance of your life on earth is an important part of your prayer today and gratitude is your joyful companion. After praying with the reflection below, I encourage you to honor the moment of your conception in some way. Your journal may be helpful here: use poetry, prayer, prose, paintings. Let your creativity flow.*

The One from whom I came chose my parents—perhaps I even had something to say about the choice. I can't remember those "before the womb" moments. Yet somehow in God's divine plan I was part of this glorious unfolding. I say "Yes" to that moment now. "Yes" to the parents to whom I was born.

I do not know the circumstances of my conception. Human life is frail and parents are not perfect. I may have been conceived in a moment of tender love, or my conception may have been less noble. Today I look upon the frailty of my father and mother and I forgive them any flaw that they may have had at the moment of my conception. I cannot be born fully until I am able to forgive.

On this day I thank my mother and father for the gift of my life. Part of this day I will live in joyful gratitude for my parents.

Since I am now able to love and forgive I will send blessings of love to them wherever they are. Having done this I return to the moment of my conception and pray with that moment and abide in it.

Dear Author of Life, this day I was conceived in my mother's womb. Although I cannot remember this moment, in my mind's eyes I climb into the scene. I dwell there in this season of becoming. I embrace my beginning of life on earth. My father's seed, searching for life, finds a home in the waiting egg in my mother's womb. This is my beginning. I am listening to this moment. I hear you saying, "Before I formed you in the womb I knew you." In this moment of prayerful remembering, I place my trust in you. I know that you used the sacred, earthy moment of my conception to fulfill your divine design for my presence in this world. It was not an empty moment. It was a moment of grace and glory. I enshrine this moment of my beginning on my banner and in my journal. I gaze on it with gratitude as I pray. Amen.

Day 4

*You shaped my inmost self
carefully and tenderly.
You joyfully wove me together
in my mother's womb.*

Read Psalm 139:13-18

> *Spend this day in the womb. You're not ready to be born yet. You are slowly growing into a little baby. Your body is being formed in miraculous ways. Everything about you is a miracle. The umbilical cord is not yet cut. You are one with your mother and you are being nourished through her body. Somehow in the great mystery of things your father's life blood also flows through you. In the midst of it all, God dwells! God tenderly cradles your becoming.*

There in the dark and earthy chapel of my mother's womb I was given the gift of life. A breath of life was breathed into me from the great Source of Life I call God. I cannot remember that moment, but I claim and own it as good. There in that dark, holy, and nurturing chapel of my mother's womb the Author of Life held me and began to shape me. I was so tiny. For nine months I grew. Under the eye of God, in the womb of my mother, with the encouragement of my father and friends, I grew.

It is possible that there in the security of the womb, I picked up noisy, disturbing vibes from the outer world. Unrest, discontent, sadness, fear that existed in my home might have drifted into my small being even before I was born. I gaze upon my tiny form and wonder what I experienced there in the comforting darkness of the womb. Did the fears of the world reach me there? Did the hope and expectation of my arrival give joy to those who waited for me?

Dear Caretaker, my loving Mother and Father, through the power of Jesus who was lifted up on the cross and through the power of many faith-filled people who continue to be lifted up on the cross, free me of any anxiety and turbulence that might have affected my life before my birth. In the womb, I wait. I wait for the moment of birth. I am a bit reluctant to leave this warm cave, where I have lived for nine months, and enter into the mystery of the unknown. I trust you now at the hour of my birth. My birth is also a little death. O God, I trust you. I trust you to carry me lovingly into this fearful, beautiful land of life. Take hold of my hand on this day of my birth. Amen.

Day 5

*You lifted me out of the womb,
singing me the song of my life.
You took me by the hand
and became my teacher.*

Read Psalm 22:10-11

> *On this fifth day of retreat you will be celebrating your birthday. This is a very important day for you and I encourage you to think of creative ways to receive this day as part of God's unfolding plan for you and for your world. Make plans for a celebration. The first part of the day might be just the quiet, prayerful joy of embracing your moment of birth. Toward the end of the day you may wish to invite a few friends to celebrate in some special way—a birthday party!*

I am still in the womb, yet I must come forth. The time has come for me to be born. I am afraid of birth. The womb is so comfortable. It is a nurturing place. It is my home. I am leaving my first home. Leaving is not easy. Already I feel the trauma of coming into an unfamiliar land. Do I really want to be born? Do I have a choice? Am I being called to birth?

I receive the moment of my birth as the glorious moment it truly was. I put myself in the delivery room. I am the child being born. I am listening to my own birth cry—the sacred scream of life. This is my first birth. There will be many others.

I rest in my mother's arms. My father and other loving people are excited about my arrival. Their smiles fall on me like sunshine. I say to myself what every child needs to hear. (What would that be for you?) Psalm 139 comes to mind and I keep praying over and over again, "O God, a wonder am I!" I look at myself as a gift of God and I whisper, "Happy Birthday!"

Beloved Creator, heal me of any trauma that may have occurred at birth. Let me never forget that you were present at my birth, encouraging me, nudging me, drawing me out of the womb, feeling the birth pains with me. May this birth be a symbol of my first act of obedience. With immense gratitude I look upon this moment and say "Yes" to life. Amen.

Day 6

In the clouds a rainbow appears,
a sign of everlasting friendship
between the Creator and the created.
When life starts limping
look to the rainbow and remember.

Read Genesis 9:12-17

> *These are the days, the weeks after your birth. Try to image*
> *yourself in this new and strange world. Ask those who were*
> *with you to give you details about your birth and the place*
> *where you spent your first days, weeks, months. Behold your*
> *tiny hands and feet. Be excited about your own birth. It is*
> *a way of receiving and accepting your place in the world.*
> *Think of yourself today as a gift, a rainbow, a sign of hope.*

A rainbow in the sky is God's promise of hope for us. On these days of rejoicing, the days after my birth, I remember the rainbow that I am to God and to the world. I celebrate the happy memories of my birth. The poet Rabindranath Tagore suggests that every time a child is born into this world it comes bearing a message of joy. And this is the message: *God is not discouraged!* Today I muse over this truth. My birth announces to the world: *God still has hope. This new child is the proof.*

I remember the baptismal waters and I am filled with peace. I imagine the church of my baptism and feel the waters flowing over me. Will I be a rainbow in my family? My church? My world? Am I willing to be in process, always on the edge of new growth? Will I grow up with an open heart?

As a reminder of my baptism I fill a bowl with water. I create some ritual with the water. It may be a simple sprinkling of my room or just dipping my hands into the water in memory of being immersed into Christ. I sign myself with the sign of the cross.

O Christ rising from the baptismal font, hold me and behold me. Behold my life. Let your cleansing waters wash over me. I want to be there again in that moment, small and free, innocent and bright. My baptismal day is another birthday; I can ask for any gift I want. For this new birthday I ask for vision. Give me eyes that are far-seeing and tender, that I might see beyond the masks that others wear, all the way through to their deep-down goodness. Give me the ability to see with my heart that I might be able to discern the mysteries of life. Teach me to be a source of refreshment for others. Amen.

Day 7

I have relied on you since I was born.

Read Psalm 71:1-8

> *Allow yourself to be small today. As you pray, invite your
> dependence on God and others to rest in your heart. Let this
> be a day of envisioning what it was like in your home those
> first weeks after your birth. It was a time in your life when
> you had to rely on others. You had no choice. Someone had
> to care for you. Remember those who cared for you as a
> child. In your mind's eye put a frame around the faces that
> appear to you. Let each face be an icon for you, a sacred
> image to gaze upon. Whose faces are these? Pray for them
> now. And if an image should appear of someone who hurt
> you as a child, use your far-seeing, tender eyes that your look
> might become a prayer of compassion. Hold on to God's
> hand and begin to forgive.*

I awaken today with wonder, still singing through my small
being, "A wonder am I!" I am living through the first weeks in
my new home. Everything is so big and I am so small.
Brokenness and beauty are all around me. Every day for the rest
of my life will be a birthday. I want to be open to that truth so
that I will be ready to be born again each day.

What was my life like those first hours and days? Did I feel
safe in the presence of my family? Was I born into a warm and
nurturing home? Was I born into a broken home? In a way, every
home is a broken home because we are a broken people and we are
born into a broken world, but was there a special kind of brokenness in my home caused by addictive behavior, excessive poverty,
selfishness, greed, or insufficient love? If so, I embrace this

brokenness as part of who I am. I do not turn away from it or deny it. I embrace the brokenness saying, "This, too, is a part of my life!"

O Great Lover of Broken Things, mend what is torn and tattered in my life. Reach out with your hand and touch my broken places. How often your hand reached out with healing graces in the gospels. I need your healing touch again. In the stillness of this moment I imagine that I am holding your hand. I am trusting you with my life. I am blessing those who reached out to me when I was small and helpless. Bless them with me. Open my eyes that I may see how good it is to trust you. Open my heart that I may not be ashamed to depend on you. I have relied on you since my birth. Amen.

Day 8

I have no food but tears day and night.

Read Psalm 42

> *One of the ways to let the "big people" in your house know that you needed or wanted something during this fragile time in your life was through your tears. It may seen strange to spend a day praying with tears, but that's what I'm asking you to do. Tears are, indeed, a gift. If there are tears in you that need to be released, make a gentle effort to free them this day. Ask God for the gift of tears. Invite them and welcome them. Remember your past tears. Pray for those who have no tears.*

The weeks go by slowly. I have been born into a lovely, yet complicated and fallible world. I wonder about my first months. What were they like? Did I cry a lot? I sit quietly and listen to myself cry. It was my way of letting my needs be known. How did those around me feel when I cried? Did they listen to my cries with reverence? Did I make them nervous? Did they attend to my needs to shut me up? Did they let me cry too long? Did they neglect me or did they overly pamper me? Did I truly experience being loved? Today I spend some time in the arms of forgiveness. I want to forgive any neglect I may have suffered in my early life.

With tenderness I focus on my baby tears. I hear myself crying. I receive those tears unashamed. With the psalmist I pray, "I have no food but tears day and night." How many times have I felt that way? I ponder. Do I have tears stored away that need to flow? Since the inhibition and freedom of my childhood is gone, do I try to hide my tears? If there are hidden tears within me, I give them my attention now. I give them permission to water my life with their healing presence. I pray with the tears deep inside.

Jesus, take the tears stored in the depths of my soul and unite them to your own tears. I see you weeping at the tomb of Lazarus. I see you weeping above the walls of Jerusalem. I see Mary Magdalene weeping and washing your feet with her tears. I see Peter weeping bitterly for having denied you. Your tears and the tears of your friends give me hope. It takes both rain and sun to make a rainbow. Give me the gift of tears. Amen.

Day 9

*In my weakness
I discover my strength.*

Read 2 Corinthians 12:9-10

> *What do you think you learned in the womb? Ponder the wisdom of the womb. Is there anything that you unconsciously learned in the womb that you need to relearn? Were you perhaps born with some innate wisdom that you've forgotten? This could be powerful content for your meditation today. The womb was your first home. You were nurtured there for nine months. Taking a backward glance now, how was the womb a teacher for you? Henry David Thoreau once said that he was forever regretting that he was not as wise as he was on the day he was born. I was startled when I first came upon these words. However, after much reflection on them, I feel closer to understanding what he meant. Reflect on these things today.*

My sojourn in the womb was a time of grace. I was totally open to receiving each part of my body as it slowly grew. I didn't try to make anything grow faster. I was patient. I could wait. All was gift. I was nourished and nurtured. I possessed nothing except what I needed.

As I look at my small frame these first months of my life, I reflect on the wisdom of the womb. Did I come forth from the womb wise? I think so. The wisdom that I must learn to embrace is that I came from the womb poor. There lies the reason for my wisdom. It was the only time in my life when I didn't fight my poverty. I didn't fight my tears, my hungers, my fears. I let them be known. I was poor with a poverty that made me rich. I had nothing and let it be known. I was totally dependent and unashamed of my need.

Jesus, I embrace those very early months of my life today. I embrace them with the same reverence that you embrace my poverty and littleness. Restore the poverty of my childhood so that once again I can rest trustingly in the shadow of your wings, waiting to be fed, expecting to be fed, and crying out to you in my need. Through the power of your own emptiness, Jesus, heal me of any unnecessary scars left over from the poverty of my childhood. Let me taste the richness of that poverty once again. Amen.

Day 10

*Covering his feet with kisses
she anointed them
with her love and ointment.*

Read Luke 7:36-38

> *Try to envision the people who might have held you when
> you were a baby. Touch is essential for wholesome living and
> growth. When touch is healthy it is a sacrament of God's
> presence. Let this be a day to focus on the gift of human
> touch. Be conscious of all that you touch today whether it be
> people or things. Practice awareness. Hold all things as
> though they were sacred vessels.*

Days, weeks, months are going by. It is the springtime of my
life. I am unfolding like a new bud. I am learning to see, to
move, to crawl, to walk, to talk, to smile and laugh, to touch. I
am becoming aware. It is a very fragile time in my life. I am vulnerable. I am more sensitive than most people realize.

I close my eyes and dream a little. Loving arms surround me.
The touch of human hands is healing the loneliness of leaving
the womb. The touch of human flesh enfolding me helps me to
feel safe in my new home. Touch is so important at this age. I
know now that babies can die from lack of touch. Human touch
is meant to be healing.

I focus now on all the people who held me when I was
small. I see myself lovingly passed around like a treasure. I am
being anointed with the gift of human touch. My cheek is
against my mother's. She is humming softly. I see myself sitting
on my father's lap. I hear the stories he tells me. How many
hands I've passed through: parents, grandparents, friends,
brothers, sisters, and relatives. I stop now for a moment of

communion with all those who held me in my early years. I inscribe their names in my journal. Spending a few moments in communion with them, I look on each of them with love. In a spiritual way I touch them again.

Having fondly remembered those who held me in my early years, I remember also the woundedness of the human condition. My parents owned the same frail human flesh that is mine and so there were times when I longed for a loving touch that I didn't receive. There were times when I wanted to be held and mom was too busy. Sometimes she was holding someone else— a new baby perhaps—and I felt jealous and rejected. Sometimes she was sick; she couldn't care for me. I felt scared, abandoned. There were times when I needed the strong protective arms of a father around me, but my father wasn't there. He was always working; or, perhaps he didn't feel comfortable with touching. He was too preoccupied, too busy to touch, and so a part of me yearned for a love I never experienced. I may have come from a home where one parent was absent because of divorce or death. There was a big hole in my home. That hole moved to my heart and so there is a wound that needs to be healed.

Some touches I received were not healing touches. There are memories tucked inside me and wrapped in question marks. I may have been abused by people trapped in their own misery. Perhaps I was spanked for reasons I didn't understand, for things I didn't do. A part of me still faintly remembers being pushed away with anger or impatience when I wanted something at the wrong time. As these painful moments return to my memory I invite the healing breath of God to move across my pain like a gentle wind through tall grasses. I bless these memories and continue the pilgrimage through my life.

Jesus, when you pitched your tent with us on earth, your healing touch brought many folks back to life. In memory of this touch of yours I beg you to hold close to your heart all those whose touch has enabled me to come through the scars of childhood feeling anointed and loved. I give thanks for Mary Magdalene in your life. Her anointing touch, her hands and hair and tears upon your feet must have helped to heal the ache of loneliness that you, who took on our human flesh, understand so well. Amen.

Day 11

*You journey through the desert
led by your God.
When you become hungry
God feeds you with manna.*

Read Deuteronomy 8:1-6

*What memories of hunger, unfulfilled needs, or neglect are
stored in your heart? This is a day to focus on unmet needs.
Reflecting on these instances of neglect is not to grovel in
them but rather to embrace them as part of your history.
This can also be a way of checking to see if there is any thing
you need to forgive. Is there a connection between the
hungers you feel today and the hungers you remember from
the past?*

Every human person born into this world has suffered some
neglect. The pain of neglect is locked up in our hearts
whether we realize it or not. Those who are our caretakers during our childhood are limited in many ways. Those limitations
may have brought about some kind of negligence in our lives. We
were all neglected a little. It is the human condition.

I focus now on the neglects of my early childhood and I
spend some time today praying for the ones who neglected me. I
spend time forgiving. If any particular memory comes to mind,
I ask it why it has come and listen to its answer. I embrace it and
I try to discern what it wants to teach me.

Somewhere in me there is something that didn't get fed
enough and it cries out for feeding even now. It is still hungry. I
take a long look at this *ache-of-not-enough* that lingers in my
heart. I try to name it: not enough love, not enough understanding, not enough food, not enough patience, not enough
security, not enough affirmation, not enough attention. On this

pilgrimage through life I ask God to heal, feed, and embrace this ache. I spend some time getting in touch with the *ache-of-not-enough* in my life. I write about it in my journal and look on it with understanding. I place it on my banner in some way.

Jesus, I willingly hand over to you the hungers that linger in my heart. Dress the wounds of my early childhood with your glance of life. May that glance be the manna that satisfies my hunger. As I list my deepest hungers in my journal I ask you to listen to the cries of my heart and feed me with the food I most need at this time in my life. Thank you for the hungers in my life that have encouraged me to go deeper and explore my inner life. Thank you for the hungers that have drawn me into your heart. Amen.

Day 12

The One guiding you
leads you into a country
fruitful and promising.
You are standing on the edge of a good land.
Be grateful and never forget your guide.

Read Deuteronomy 8:7-20

> *The introduction to this retreat stressed that throughout our lives we have been both bitten and blessed. Today will be a day to reflect on the blessings. This is a day of beauty. Imagine in your early years being awakened to beauty. Celebrate your awareness of beauty. Spend as much time with beautiful things as you can fit into your schedule. Walk through this day with eyes wide open. Beauty is healing. Expect good things.*

It is time to reflect on all the good things of my life. I am being led into a prosperous land, a land of streams and springs, of waters that well up from *the deep* in valleys and hills, a land of wheat and barley, of vines, a land where I will have all that I need. If my human caretakers neglected my needs because of the frailty and limitations of their lives, there was One who never neglected me. I listen to God's faithfulness as I lean into the blessings of my life.

Indeed the One who has created me has prepared a feast of life for me. Today I reflect on all my early memories of *beauty* as I imagine what it was like to see the world for the first time. These memories may not be conscious right now, but somewhere within me there was a "first time" for many moments of beauty. Each one was a little epiphany.

What was it like to see the stars the first time? Did a little bit of infinity slip into my child's heart as I beheld our star-spangled universe? Was it an epiphany, a moment of trans-formation? Did I notice the stars all by myself or was my family wise enough to hold me up to the heavens for a glimpse at the earliest moment possible?

What did my small mind think about the array of color that unfolded before me each day? The flowers! The green grass! The blue sky! The clouds! The rainbow! I visualize my first rain-drops, my first snowflakes. I think about the first time I felt my feet touch the earth. Even if I can't actually remember some of these moments in my imagination I spend time with all these pieces of beauty.

As I journal today I list some of my favorite memories of beauty from all the ages of my life. I allow myself to be fed with beauty today.

Loving God, my presence on this earth is like a long Transfiguration. You have brought me to this mountain of glory to show me your face. At times, like Peter, I want to stay here forever, but I'm slowly begin-ning to realize that I'm only a pilgrim on the earth. Each moment has its special nourishment. I breathe it in—then let it go. My life is richer for each moment of glory that I've tasted. I am grateful for all these moments of beauty with which you have blessed me throughout my life. Amen.

Day 13

Let your heart be sincere.
Be steadfast.
Don't fall apart when disaster comes.

Read Sirach 2:1-18

> *On this day of your retreat I want you to reflect on your first*
> *memories of life outside your family home—early memories*
> *of classroom days. Recall teachers and classmates. As each*
> *child or teacher stands before you, behold them briefly and*
> *then put each one into the heart of God. Wherever they may*
> *be today, ask that God's compassion and love follow them*
> *through life. You may recall someone you would like to con-*
> *tact. Write them a letter and tell them of your memories.*

It is time to leave the womb a second time. This time it is the womb of my home I must leave. There is a wresting away from my familiar daily routine as I go to school for the first time. Leaving the security and familiarity of home for the structured atmosphere of the classroom might have been a bit of a trauma. There is a part of me that is shy as I walk into this new setting. I reflect on that moment. What are my memories? Did I feel safe with this teacher? Was I comfortable with all these strange children? Was it easy to make friends or was it a fearful experience? Did I have a sense of belonging?

"It isn't fair," is a chant I learned early in life. So many things in my childhood just didn't come out even. There were teachers who seemed unfair, and some who didn't like me or understand me. Perhaps a better way of saying this is that there were teachers who, because they had not yet found the core of God within their own hearts, couldn't connect with the core of God in me. They couldn't see the need, the potential, the beauty, and the worth crying out to be born. They ignored me because I didn't stand out as a shining light, so I carried in my heart a sense of not being worthwhile. Yes, painful memories linger that come from feelings of not being seen, not being noticed. Sometimes it felt as though I just wasn't there.

On the playground the chant of, "it's not fair," continued. There were times of being punished for things I hadn't done. There were times others were punished in my stead and I didn't have the courage to own up to the fact that I was the one at fault. I reflect on the fears and pains of my early days in the classroom and I pray with the wounds that come from any kind of injustice experienced in those early years at school.

God of my early childhood, help me to live with the fact that life doesn't always come out even. I place in my heart and in yours all the people of my early childhood who come to my mind as having been unfair to me. I embrace also those who may have suffered some injustice because of me. Holding these people in my heart where you have made your home is the best way I know to pray for them. I pray, too, for those whose kindness I remember. Bless them with your loving kindness now. May it follow them throughout their lives. Amen.

Day 14

*Take one another's interests
into your heart
and give them a home.*

Read Philippians 2:1-11

Our theme for today is Belonging. Deep in our souls lives an ache—a longing to belong. We want to belong to a faith community, a family, a club, a team! We long for someone to hold our interests in their hearts. And we, too, want to reach out with loving attention to others. Each of us needs some special person in our lives—someone we can call friend. What are your early childhood memories of belonging? Where and with whom did you feel at home? What is your experience of belonging at this time in your life? Meditate today on your need to belong. How has this longing been fulfilled for you? Consider sending a card of gratitude to some of the people who have taken your interests into their hearts.

I continue to reflect on the wounds of my classroom days. Peer pressure started early. I wanted to fit in, to belong. What is necessary to belong? Who makes the rules that say, "You're OK, you've got what is required to be part of this group"? The rules are unwritten. They are subtle but they are there. They range anywhere from having the right kind of sandwich in your lunch pail to wearing clothes with the right name brand.

There are memories of times I didn't fit in—times when it seemed that no one had my interests in their heart. I wanted to be friends with someone but I was the wrong color, the wrong age, the wrong build. I wanted to play on the team but I was always chosen last. I was laughed at when I didn't come through with flying colors. Or perhaps I was one of the popular kids and I felt pressure to ignore others in order to stay part of *my group*. Deep inside, I didn't want to act this way. I knew it wasn't loving, but I didn't have the courage or the maturity to be my best self.

I spend a little time now in gratitude for those people who always seemed to have my best interests at heart—those with whom I felt safe, to whom I belonged. I extend these memories to the people in my life today.

Loving God, turn a caring eye toward all people who have been left out of the circle of love. Protect those who have been rejected and excluded. Send caring people into their lives that they may discover their beauty and goodness.

Thank you for the loving people who have been gifts in my life, those who have treated me with respect and kindness and helped me to believe in my worth. If there is anyone I have ever shut out of the circle of my love, send someone to them to remedy the harm I may have done. And for those times when I have felt excluded, I forgive to the extent I am able. By the help of your grace supply any forgiveness that is lacking in my life. Amen.

Day 15

*Fill your mind with all that is joyful,
all that is noble, authentic and beautiful.
Then God's peace will stand guard
at the doorway of your heart.*

Read Philippians 4:4-9

> *Use this day as a time to review the happiness of childhood.
> No matter what our painful stories might be, surely there are
> blessings to be remembered. Can you recall some of the joy-
> ful, authentic, and beautiful gifts of your early years? Make
> an effort to remember the good times. Who are the friends
> and mentors that linger in your thoughts today? Look upon
> this early period in your life as a school of learning. Which
> experiences stand out in your memory? Have some of the
> blessings of childhood followed you into your adult life? Let
> good memories surround you and bless you today.*

Having looked upon some of the things that have bitten me during my youth I now turn toward that which has blessed me. I take a long redemptive glance into the heart of the child I once was. How good it would be if some of the sensitivity, won-der, freedom, receptivity, and wisdom of that child could be restored in me. With gratitude I gaze upon the blessings. I have indeed been both bitten and blessed.

Once upon a time I had not fully discovered the world I live in. I have delightful memories of experiencing my world for the first time as it wondrously unveiled itself before my eyes. Day by day in little ways I remember beholding my world and behold-ing my life. Even the fears and feelings of inadequacy can't com-pletely hide the joy of discovery that belongs to a child. I rejoice, then, as I look at the blessings of young life. I take time to let the children who were part of my classroom experience be present again. Every person I have ever known is still a little part of my life, and so I try to remember their faces. I call to mind the unfolding process of learning that went on both in and out of the classroom. What a wonderful gift the mind is. I meditate on the ability to think, to ponder and dream, to calculate and decide. The creativity of my Creator is being shared with me. In countless ways my mind has been a blessing to me and to others.

My heart, too, has blessed me. I am able to care for others, to love intensely. Wonder, surprise, and gratitude are mine. I can be angry, sad, fearful. All these emotions have taught me much about myself and the world around me. To be able to feel deeply is a precious gift. That gift has been mine. I am grateful for the wide span of my emotions.

Loving God, help me never to ignore my feelings but to accept the blessings they can bring. You have filled my life to the brim. Today with eyes of the child who still lives within me, I look upon all that has blessed me: the people, the new knowledge, the sense of being nurtured, the deep feelings of sorrow and joy, the wonder of nature, the seasons that have passed over our land and the seasons of the land of my heart. Thank you for your constant presence in my growing fields. Restore in me the heart of a child as I continue growing up. Amen.

Day 16

Be my guide and teacher.
Lead me on the path of truth,
for you are a God who loves me.

Read Psalm 25

> *Use this day as a time to review your early memories of sexuality. Not all families handle sexual issues well. Young people often suffer on this mysterious and beautiful path. Today then would be a time to recall early sexual experiences and bless them as part of your school of learning. If there are things you need to express or share with someone, begin by writing your feelings in your journal.*

My childhood was pure and simple. Not many false gods were present. As I grow older I am able to make choices. It is now that a new challenge in life begins. Adolescence can be a lonely time.

I am so aware of my body these days. It speaks to me in demanding ways that I can't ignore. It has certainly gotten my attention. I have been told that I am a temple of the Holy Spirit. If this is so, then I would like to discover all I can about this earthy temple of God. But the fact remains that I can't find anyone who seems truly *at home* in this temple.

I am maturing sexually. I am experiencing the awakening of sexual desire. It is both frightening and delightful. I feel so alive these days, yet at times so desperately lonely. I don't know what to do with these new, powerful feelings in my body, and there's no one with whom I can comfortably talk. Much of my sex education I learn on the sidewalk, from jokes, or from magazines I have to keep hidden.

There is such an enigma linked with all this and so much fear. My parents seem as fearful as I. Thus, the sacred mystery and gift of sexuality often gets lost in confusion. Sometimes it is presented as something ugly—surely not a subject to talk about in the family. Sexual feelings are often considered sinful. So where do I go with all my questions? Sometimes I go nowhere. Keeping all this in mind, it is quite understandable why I may have moved into my adult years with unhealthy and confused attitudes about my sexuality.

As my body wakes up I begin to wonder where my soul is hiding. There are strange gods lurking in me, vying for my devotion. These are days of deep questioning. My heart is often wrapped in question marks. My trust level is low and most of my questions remain unasked. My values are being formed. It is a time of juggling values and trying to understand who I am. There are times when I do not measure up to expectations—my own and those of my family and friends. I want to fit in with the crowd, but to fit in I have to sacrifice another part of myself—an honest part that is struggling to express the truth of who I am.

Peer pressure continues. It is such a monster clawing at my throat, sapping me of my life's strength. I want to be popular—to be part of the crowd! Loved. Desired. Appreciated. Noticed. Yet often I feel invisible—a beauty unseen. I begin to doubt myself.

Jesus, as I bring to mind this vulnerable time in my life, allow me to experience your abiding presence in the midst of the turmoil. Now in my adult life I begin to see my sexuality as a sacrament of love and vibrant energy, a gift from God. Bless the people I may have hurt in past years because of my insecurity, immaturity, or insensitivity. Heal me from all the ways I've suffered from lack of adequate sex education. Help me to grow fully into a healthy and alive sexual being. For any sexual abuse that I may have received or given, I ask for your healing and forgiveness. Amen.

Day 17

*You are to be a brand new person
created in God's image.
No more masks!*

Read Ephesians 4:22-32

*Reflect on growing pains today. The difficult and exciting
years of adolescence offer many blessings, but they can be
confusing times as well. It is always difficult being sus-
pended between childhood and adulthood. Pray with your
memories of growing up, both in your family household and
in the world about you. Let today be a day for embracing
the "prodigal" parts of your life. Spend time with family
scars—quarrels, misunderstandings, grudges, jealousies that
have never been dealt with. These times may have been
growing pains and blessings in disguise. However, they
never feel like blessings when we are going through these difficult stages of growth. What are the "run-away" times in
your life that you need to pray with? Where have your hiding places been? How have you felt lost and unseen?*

The blessings of my youth still fresh in my memory, I continue
my journey through the fields of growth. Growing up is never
easy. I'm not exactly a child anymore but I'm not an adult either.
I'm somewhere between childhood and adulthood. "In-between"
is a difficult place to be. I'm at that age when I often feel misunderstood. I'm confused about life. I want answers that adults
seem unable to give me. I struggle with relationships in my
family. I feel rivalry. Sometimes I am jealous.

I recall the story of Joseph, the favorite son of Jacob who was
given a coat of many colors. What is the "Joseph's coat" of my

childhood—the gift never received but longed for? Or, perhaps the gift received that brought the envy and jealousy of others? (Genesis 37:3-4)

There were parents, brothers, and sisters who didn't understand me. I never felt discovered. There was a part of me that didn't seem to fit. I kept going more and more into a shell to hide my fears. I became fearful of expressing myself. I feared rejection. Or, perhaps I hid my anxieties by becoming loud and jovial. I put on the mask of a clown. It was easier that way, but I was hiding all the same. Something was crying out from behind the mask wanting to be known and loved, but I just didn't know how to take the mask off. Maybe I'm still wearing it today.

I embrace also the prodigal part of my youth. I have at times been wasteful with my inheritance. I've squandered the love of God and the love of others. Gathering up the seeming wasted moments of my rebellious days, I forgive myself the waste. Now I behold it all as rich compost from which new growth comes. All of this was a learning season in my life.

I reflect on my run-away times—those times when I actually did run away or when I wanted to run away. Perhaps I had some healthy run-away places—places where I went when life got too confusing. There were quarrels in my home that I didn't want to hear. There were times when I tried to bring about peace in my family and was misunderstood. There were times when I cared so deeply about everyone, but didn't know how to show it. And so, sometimes I "took to the woods or the streets," because I needed a hiding place, a place to go where I could try to understand, or where someone outside my family might understand me. I reflect on my hiding places of long ago. I slip quietly into one of them in my memory and I pray.

O God of my youth, return. Return to this hiding place with me. Let me experience in a new way the healing balm of your presence. Give me confidence in myself at last. Touch my insecurities with your courage. Show me your loving kindness. O Savior of those who flee, hide me in the shadow of your wings. You see me as I am for you are a God of no-masks. With firm and gentle hands remove the protective masks I wear. Mend the scared and scarred places in my life that I may put on the new self, created in your image. Amen.

Day 18

*Do not be afraid
for I have hold of you.
My cherished possession, you are.
Your name I love.*

Read Isaiah 43:1-5

> *Today I ask you to dwell on that transitional time of moving into young adulthood from adolescence. What are memories of your faith life at this time? How was God a part of your life during your high-school and college years? What issues surfaced for you during these years? Spend time pondering your past and present images of God beginning with childhood images. Let this journey take you through various stages of development. Who is God for you today? What images of God are most comfortable for you? Spend time yearning for the God who has journeyed with you all these years.*

As I grow into a young adult I begin to realize that growing up has very little to do with age. Feelings and issues from childhood and adolescence never dealt with continue to show up in my life.

The strong need for love, appreciation, affection, acceptance have stayed with me. The same fears and anxieties still plague me. The demand and drive for success seem stronger than ever. At times I am overwhelmed, wondering if I am ever going to succeed in today's fast lane. Choosing a career holds so much uncertainty. It's acceptable to be afraid when I'm little—but what about when I'm growing up? Is it still acceptable? What do I do with my feelings now? Many of my feelings are locked away. They used to be my friends, but now I've buried them deep inside to avoid getting hurt. Much of the honesty of my child-hood is somewhere in storage waiting to be rediscovered. My childhood inhibitions are waiting to be set free.

And where was God in all of this? What are my remem-brances of God's presence? Who has God been for me in all the ages of my life? How have my images of God changed over the years? Quieting my mind, I recall the God who has journeyed with me through childhood, on into adolescence and into my young adult years. I muse on the many faces of God. Which of these images do I resonate with today:

> . . . a Father providing me with all that I need,
> . . . a Mother rocking me in her arms,
> . . . a shepherd who finds me no matter where I wander,
> . . . a lamb of God whose blood is poured out for me,
> . . . an eagle teaching her young to fly,
> . . . a king sitting on a throne ruling the world with justice,
> . . . an angry parent who punishes my disobedience,
> . . . a ray of sunlight piercing through a thick mist,
> . . . a windy-fiery Spirit hovering over my life, inflaming me with energy and love,
> . . . a holy invisible power that silently breathes green into the trees and grass,
> . . . a piece of my heart that can't stop loving,
> . . . a friend who calls me by name,
> . . . a loving Lord bending down to wash my feet,
> . . . the person of Jesus who affirms and heals me?

O Lord of all the ages, God of many names and faces, even when I was turning my eyes toward other gods you continued to look steadily upon me with an eye of love. You have always been revealing your name to me. In countless ways you have shown me your face. Even in my rebellious, wayfaring days you were there beside me, seeing me not as I looked to human eyes, but seeing me as I really was—seeing to the core of my being. Keep on seeing me. Continue to reveal your name to me. Show me your face that I may have hope. Move freely in my life. Do not allow me to block your presence in any way. No matter what age I am, I always want to be willing to grow up again. Grow up in me and keep calling my name. Amen.

Day 19

An inheritance
is being kept safe for you.
It is stored in the heavens,
it will never rust or fade.
It is your birth into hope.
It will endure.

Read 1 Peter 1:3-9

> *Success! Failure! What is your understanding of success?*
> *List successes in your journal. These need not be as impres-*
> *sive as climbing Mt. Everest. What are the successes in life*
> *that you overlook? Who have been your mentors and*
> *guides: those who have helped you find meaning? What*
> *books have been instrumental in shaping your life? On this*
> *day, when you are reflecting on your successes, take some*
> *time also to remember real or imagined failures. What*
> *have you learned from them? This is a day to pray with*
> *your successes and failures.*

In my young adult life the gnawing ache for love continues. However, sometimes the drive for success and my competitive spirit hide my vulnerability. But when no one is watching it comes and stands before me like a sentinel bearing a silent message.

There are times when I hide my desire to be loved behind a wall of indifference. However, if I am open to conversion in my life I will discover behind that wall—underneath that mask—a beautiful and wise person, perhaps a successful person too. I see my successes best when I don't compare myself with others. I am beautifully unique and wiser than I know myself to be. The wisdom of the womb is still with me. The receptive child who is not afraid to live with open hands is still very much alive in the depths of my being. These are all gifts—rich qualities that need to be claimed. I must learn how to give back to that child its wings. Perhaps then success will wear a different face.

There is, of course, the success that I longed for but have not experienced. I often feel the ache of failure. I've learned to evaluate my self-worth by how much I accomplish. There is a drive to *do* rather than to *be*. I've never given myself permission to relax. Maybe I need to learn how to loiter a bit in my life—to be idle. Or perhaps the success that I have experienced in my professional career has damaged my family life, my community life, or my personal relationships. No matter how successful I've been there is still the gnawing ache that something is not right.

O God of Abundant Life, on some days there is an emptiness in me that feels like a bottomless pit. I have tried to fill this emptiness with everything: work/activities, possessions, alcohol, sex, people/relationships, drugs, sports, TV entertainment, books/knowledge. The list could go on and on. The emptiness remains. I know now that St. Augustine was right. My heart will never find rest until it rests in you. Truly, you are my inheritance, my sure ray of hope. Enter my restlessness that I may find success by resting in you. Amen.

Day 20

*Long before the world came to be,
God's eye was on me.
I was destined in Christ to be holy.*

Read Ephesians 1:1-14

> *Contemplate your relationship with the church. What was growing up in the church like for you? How has the church healed or hurt you? Pray today about your memories of being part of a faith community. Meditate on your call to be holy. What does a holy life mean to you? Do you want to be a saint?*

I am listening to God's call for me to be holy. I'm a little afraid of that call. If I surrender to God's plan for me there is much that will need to change in my life. As I grow older I hear the call more deeply. Actually the call is kind of embarrassing. To how many people can I comfortably say out loud, "I want to be a saint"?

I reflect today on the church, the body of Christ on earth. In the church the call to be holy is nurtured and encouraged. In the church, too, I have experienced pain. It may be a pain about a church that once seemed too strict, more concerned about rules than persons. There may be memories of priests, sisters, ministers, or other teachers who were insensitive to me. They may even have precipitated my withdrawing from the church. If it seems that I was driven from the church, now is the time to forgive and accept healing. Actually, no one drove me from the church. I chose to leave.

Maybe the pain is because a church in which I once felt at home changed too fast. I was made to feel as though all that I was taught in the past was wrong. Devotions which once gave me great comfort were taken away and nothing replaced them. I felt sadly abandoned by a church I once loved.

My pain may have come because I thought the church was changing too fast; or I may have experienced discouragement because the church seemed so slow to change. Whatever the pain—it is real. It hurts.

Jesus, Shepherd of all ages, continue to shepherd me. I have heard your call to be a saint in the framework of this church, in spite of its sins and imperfections. I also hear your call to challenge the church and encourage it to be open and flexible, to be all that it can be. Heal me of any resentment I may be harboring against my church or its ministers. Throughout history you have chosen to lead us as a community. We come to know you through one another. May the community of churches be open to dialogue. May they be teachers for one another. I embrace this fragile community as it attempts to be your body upon the earth. The body of Christ! This is who we are. Encourage us to be all that we can be. O Christ, be at the center of all our communities. Journey with us. Amen.

Day 21

You have died to yourself
and your life is hidden in Christ.

Read Colossians 3:1-4

> *Anyone who is seriously trying to live an intentional life of*
> *transformation and growth experiences a lot of "daily*
> *dying." This is a day to reflect on the transformational deaths*
> *along your journey through life. Every death is a little birth.*
> *What are your memories of letting go? Ponder this kind of*
> *dying today.*

Death! It is all around me. It is within me. The grain of wheat is falling into the ground at every moment. It is the great healing facilitating a new birth. The reason I embrace moments of death is because I want to be transformed. My transformation gives glory to God. My transformation gives glory to the entire people of God, the church. With Jesus I say, "It was for this very reason that I have come to this hour." I reflect now on the variety of deaths I have experienced. All death is a letting go. In that letting go I am born anew. Am I truly able to let go?

> . . . I let go of my cherished opinions and I am able to listen attentively to another person.
>
> . . . I let go of my resentments so that my negative energy need never damage someone else's life or my own.
>
> . . . I let go of the fears that paralyze me so there may be more room for love in my life.
>
> . . . I let go of a loved one in death so that the Great Spirit may receive that person eternally. Holding on to someone who has died is a kind of refusal to give them back to God. Frantic clinging is not the same as healthy grieving.

. . . I let go of a relationship because I am finally able to admit that the time has come for each of us to grow in different ways. I hear Jesus saying, "Unless I go the Spirit cannot come." I understand this more clearly than ever as I painfully turn away from a destructive, smothering relationship. Unless we go from each other, the Spirit cannot come to us in new ways.

As I learn to embrace these daily deaths I am set free a little more with every death. A bit of daily dying is a great preparation for my final death. How will I die today?

Jesus, today I am the grain of wheat. I am falling into the ground and dying. I hold in memory the many deaths of my life: cherished opinions, grudges, my own will, attachments to things and to people, successes, jobs, my health, relationships I thought I couldn't live without. And finally the great letting go—the death of beloved ones going home to eternal glory. In letting them go I hand them over to the great transfiguration—the great healing. Slowly I name each death as I put it on the cross with Jesus. I see faint shades of the glory that will come from these deaths and I pray with you on the cross, "It was for this very reason that I have come to this hour." Amen.

Day 22

Death, where is your sting?

Read 1 Corinthians 15:50-58

Today you will continue with the theme of death. As you began this retreat you spent a number of days reflecting on your birth. Since it is as natural to die as it is to be born, it seems appropriate to include some time to meditate on death. Monastics who follow the rule of St. Benedict are asked to keep death daily before their eyes. St. Benedict does not mean for his monks to do this in a gloomy sort of way. It is more of a reality check. The breath that you have borrowed from the Great Spirit will some day be drawn back into God—not only your breath, but the breath of all your loved ones.

Consider death today. Live this day as if it were your last day on earth. If there is something you've been wanting to say to someone, say it today. If there is something in your life you've been wanting to surrender, surrender it today. Reflect also on your loved ones who have died. Have you handed them over to God? Clinging to someone who has died only binds them and you.

Of course some deaths are more difficult to deal with than others. When death comes in tragic and unexpected ways there is no time for preparation. Sometimes these untimely deaths shock us so that we never get around to doing our grief work. This may especially be true when someone takes their own life. I have come to believe that we must learn to honor that person's decision even though we cannot comprehend it. Honoring it means we accept that which we don't understand, believing that the One from whom we have come is larger than life or death and can receive even the things we cannot grasp.

Today I lift upon the cross all the deaths of my life. The knife of separation is a sharp one. It has pierced my heart many a time. I pray with the separation of death. The loved one of my life may have died after much suffering, and so my heart is raw not only from the loss, but also from the helplessness I felt in not being able to relieve the suffering. The death may have been so sudden and unexpected that I had no time to prepare. It may have been a tragedy, a suicide, or an accident. I now name this death, remembering that death is a transition. I pray with this transition. I let go. I do not want to hold on in unhealthy ways. My loved one is asking my permission to make this transition, asking me to allow this death. (A personal example of this in my own life is the death of my little sister. I was young when she died and I began to realize years later that although God had received her, I had never handed her over. My conscious giving her to God was a completion of the grief process for me.)

And so, I honor each death, and embrace all the loved ones in my life who have died. If I have not allowed myself the luxury of grief, I try to do that today. I pray my tears. Or, my difficulty may be that I cannot let go of my grief and get on with life. If this is the case, I take a look at what is holding me back. Was I perhaps not separate enough from these loved ones while they were still with me in the flesh? Perhaps I need to pray that I am able to find my own individuality. There is something about each of us that is painfully and joyfully separate in life. We can never be totally one with another person. This, too, is a lesson I must learn in the school of life.

I take out time to reflect on my own death as well. How do I feel about dying?

Jesus, you are the resurrection and the life. Death is the great and final healing; but with my limited vision I am not always able to embrace the mystery of death. Teach me not to fear the other side of life. May it be a passing over to the sacred shore where I will see you face to face. Remind me, through remembrance, to stay in touch with my loved ones who have died. I embrace both the bite and the blessing of death. Amen.

Day 23

We are God's work of art, created in Christ Jesus
to live the good life as from the beginning
he had meant us to live it.

Read Ephesians 2:4-10

> *Since you practiced dying yesterday, you can practice the fruits of that dying today. And the fruit, of course, is abundant life. I want you to try to live this day almost as though you died and went to heaven. These next days of your retreat are going to be days of splendor, days of renewal! It is time to look at yourself with the eyes of God, the artist. Behold your life. Behold yourself as a masterpiece of God's design. The interesting thing about this assignment is that you might find it more difficult than you found reflecting on your pain or weaknesses. Most of us are not very comfortable with our virtues. The truth is that we are much dearer than we are able to acknowledge.*

God, our Creator, is an artist. I am God's work of art. I want to see myself as I truly am in God's eyes, the unfolding joy of all creation. I gaze at my beauty and the beauty that surrounds me and see the reflection of my Creator. My potential for growth is a precious gift. Daring to lift the veil of life, I see my own goodness, love, and compassion. God's love and tenderness for me is so visible today. I am allowing myself to see. Today will be a day of glory.

The bites in my life—the brokenness and the pain—are realities. The blessings are too. Brokenness and blessedness cannot be entirely separated, nor should they be. They are two sides of the same coin. Now is my moment of blessing. The splendor and glory that I try so hard to deny stand before me seeking my acceptance. If the truth be known, it is not my weaknesses that I fear; it is my virtues. My virtues fill me with hesitancy. They call me to live as the work of art that I am. They reveal to me that I am to live in God's image.

Yes, I am created in the image of God and have memories of times when, in truth, I have been faithful to that image. (Pause now and touch some of those memories.) I have been a blessing in the lives of others and I want to continue to be a blessing. God created me to be a blessing. That is such a lovely thought. Perhaps I should spend more time remembering that the seed of all the virtues has already been planted in me by my Creator. I need to help God with the growing of these seeds. I have to do my part. Today I will continue to remember my friendliness and joy, my hope and faith, my courage and trust. They are all present in the depth of my soul. I must learn to feed and nurture them.

Loving Creator, I have no quarrel with the way you have so carefully designed me in your image. Truly I am your work of art. Take me deeper today. Show me my virtues—the wonders of your design for my life. Help me not to be afraid to look into the depths of myself and believe in what I see—for I am the work of your hands. If I can believe in what I see, then I can rejoice in what I see. Precious in your sight, I am your work of art. Continue to create me in your image. Amen.

Day 24

On barren heights, rivers flow,
Out of dry ground,
springs of water gush forth.

Read Isaiah 41:17-18

> *Let this day of your retreat be a renewal, a little Lent. Pray with the symbol of water and try to remember baptismal moments in your life—times when you have been refreshed and renewed by God's grace. Image living rivers of grace flowing through your desert places. Today is also a day to dwell on God's personal love for you. Let the scripture passages offered to you speak of the tenderness of God.*

Today I remember the many ways I have been made new. Baptism is a part of my memory. I pray with those moments of being dipped into eternity, made new, watered with life.

My symbol of blessing today is water. I remember the watering holes of my life, places where I have been refreshed, cleansed, healed, and renewed. What are the events, places, and experiences—the Lents, the Easters, and the Feasts that have renewed me? They may range anywhere from the baptismal font, to an experience of reconciliation, to a favorite lake or stream where my spirit is soothed, to a well (symbolic or otherwise) in my own back yard. In my mind's eye I return to these baptismal places, these watering holes. I relive those memories.

I begin with the baptismal font and cherish again the moment when I was drenched with Christ. I dwell there. I move on to other baptismal experiences—moments of awakening and renewal. Within each of these I abide, cherishing myself as God's unfolding work of art.

I hear the voice of God whispering to me, ". . . you are precious in my eyes and glorious, and . . . I love you" (Isaiah 43:4).

I make an effort to really hear God's voice. Indeed, it is a blessing to be able to believe that I am cherished by God. I will write this blessing in my journal today—the benediction of God's personal love for me. This is the blessing I will hold in my heart as I listen to the voice of the Beloved telling me that I am carved on the palm of his hands (Isaiah 49:16).

Today I ponder deeply and try to believe from within that God's love for me is immense and personal. Again I hear the divine voice whispering to me: You are precious in my eyes and I love you!

The experience of the love of God becomes even more powerful as I allow the words of the prophet Hosea to enter my soul. In listening to the words God spoke to Israel, I change Israel's story to my own and I am touched anew by this voice of tenderness.

> When you were a child, I loved you. I called you out of slavery. Yet the more I called you the further you drew away. I was the one who taught you to walk. It was I who took you in my arms; I drew you with human cords, with bands of love. I fostered you like an infant. I raised you to my cheek. Yet, though I stooped to feed you, my child, you did not know that I was your healer. (Hosea 11:1-4 adapted)

Indwelling One, O God of Tenderness, with each baptismal renewal you are born again in the depths of my soul. I welcome the special way you are born in me today. I have been afraid of your anointing presence. I have feared my own goodness that is being etched into me each day by your gentle hands. But now in the quiet of this meditation time I look at my renewed heart with gladness. I rejoice over all my baptismal moments and I inscribe them in my journal as cherished blessings.

You have cared for me since my birth. What a mysterious being I am, for the more I am loved the further away I seem to turn. Today I say, "No more!" No more will I look away from your compassionate love. I settle quietly into this moment to contemplate your love for me. I surrender to your will. I let you love me. Your pursuing love has shaped me into your work of art. Amen.

Day 25

Receive all the virtues that God offers then wrap them round with love.

Read Colossians 3:12-17

> *Reflect today on your potential to love. We have been told that the greatest commandment is to love God with all our hearts, all our minds, all our souls, and to love our neighbor as our self. Very simply, this is a day to ask, "Am I being a lover? How well do I love?" It's a day for remembering that love is the greatest gift.*

Because God says to me, ". . . you are precious and glorious in my eyes, and I love you" (Isaiah 43:4), I am able to say the same to others. God's love for me enables me to love others. God, seeing the splendor in me, helps me to see the splendor in others. Today I meditate on my own ability to love. My power to love is immense. It is a power that comes from God, a gift that comes from the grace of being created in the image of God. I claim this gift that it may become more visible in my life.

Even if I am someone who does not love very well because I am too busy, too fearful, too bitter, or too closed, today I press the pause button of my life and gaze knowingly into my heart. Underneath it all, yes, amidst the layers of my flesh and spirit, a sacred energy resides. It is one of my greatest resources. It is my ability to love like God. Today I spend time trying to touch that energy within. I breathe in my ability to love. Then I breathe out this gift of love envisioning it flowing out to the whole world. My love reaches all human beings, all animals and birds, the trees and flowers and plants, the meadows and lakes and all that live within them. It covers the land to the ends of the earth; everything becomes a little more sacred. Immense gratitude wells up from the depths of my soul as I give thanks for this great gift of love that God has chosen to share with me.

In my journal I inscribe the names of particular people whom I love. I remember also those whose love has healed me in countless ways. I spend some time in communion with these individuals. My remembrance of each of these dear ones becomes a silent prayer within my heart.

I remember also people from my past whom I once loved—those who, because of our different paths in life, have gone into the background of my heart. I let them be present once again. If there is a bond of love that needs rekindling I enshrine it in God's sacred heart. I gaze on it until it becomes a prayer. I wait for God's direction—then walk the path that I am shown.

O Sacred Heart of Jesus, how grateful I am for my heart of flesh— this heart that can love and hurt, this heart that can be wounded and healed. There is no gift so precious as the gift of being able to love. You have planted a seed of love in my heart. It grows and grows. Only if I deny it, fear it, or smother it with trivia does its flame grow dim; yet even then, the flame can be rekindled. O Christ of love, guard the seed of love in my life. May it grow into a burning flame of love. Protect and cherish all those with whom I have shared the fire of my love. Let me never be afraid to love. Bless those whose love has enabled me to be who I am today. Rekindle the flame of love in the hearts of all who live upon this earth. Amen.

Day 26

How awesome you are, my God!
You are dressed in glory,
you wear light as your cloak.
The clouds become your chariot;
you come to meet me on the wings of the wind.

Read Psalm 104

> *Psalm 104 is a magnificent hymn of praise for creation.*
> *Since I made it clear in our introduction to this retreat that*
> *I want you to look not only upon the things that have bit-*
> *ten, bruised, and wounded you, but also on those things*
> *that have blessed you, now is the time to muse on the bless-*
> *ing of creation. Let today be a day to remember all of the*
> *ways your spirit has been blessed and rekindled through the*
> *gift of creation. Spend more time outside or at the window.*
> *Make new memories with the gifts of creation.*

The world of nature is a *blessing* easily taken for granted. Beautiful places and treasured gifts from the universe have often been instrumental in bringing peace to my troubled being. A dew drop nestled in the heart of a green leaf can bring tears to my eyes. A majestic mountain turning autumn-gold brings prayer to my heart. A waterfall with its rushing rhythmic melody delights my tired soul. A clear, calm lake soothes my restless spirit. Golden fields of wheat and vines filled with lush purple grapes help to feed my hunger for God. The pathways in the green forest remind me of God's guidance.

In the busyness of my days, however, it is easy to let these blessings slip away unnoticed. Today I am taking notice. I am remembering

   . . . the rose shyly opening,
   . . . the fields of daisies,

. . . the tree full of goldfinches,

. . . the rainstorm making the world new,

. . . the saguaro cactus silhouetted in the morning sunrise,

. . . the bluebird on the fence post,

. . . the trees dancing in the summer breeze,

. . . the sound of the morning dove,

. . . the pair of roadrunners guarding their nest,

. . . the sun scattering the clouds,

. . . the rainbow over the barn,

. . . the leaves, touched by sunlight, making lacy shadows on the wall,

. . . grass too green to remember last summers drought.

All of these, and more, are icons in my soul's storehouse of memory.

Keeping in mind that a retreat is a time of restoration, I reflect today on all the gifts of nature that have been a renaissance for me. In my spirit I return to treasured places and treasured moments. I gather up the wealth of the past. I cherish and relive the dance of creation.

Loving Creator, I cry out with all the poets of the world, "It seems you've made the world too beautiful for me to bear." Yet I will bear it joyfully and receive its healing balm. Today my God, I am making two promises. I will find one simple blessing—one memory from the past to which I give my undivided attention. I will let it bless me again. My second promise to you, O Great Artist of this world, is this: I will also spend time in the present moment. With new eyes, I will behold some simple gift that is very near me. Keeping it company I will be renewed in its presence. Amen.

Day 27

The seventh day is uniquely holy,
for on that day after the flurry of creation
God put everything on hold and said:
Let there be rest!
The word of God is pulsing with life,
leaping with hallowed activity,
pervading the inner recesses of the soul, with clarity
it can discern the heart of things.

Read Genesis 2:1-4 and Hebrews 4:12-16

I have a two-fold task for you today. First I would like for you to consider how you have kept the "sabbath" in your lifetime. Has the encouragement to take one day a week for restoration and rest meant anything to you? Which day has been your holy day? Consider the value of having a day of rest and spiritual renewal each week. Is it hard for you to be faithful to Sunday (or your own holy day)? Has it become just another day? How might you restore its original intent? Let today be a true sabbath for you.

Second, let today be a time to take a grateful look at how the word of God has nourished you throughout your life. The Hebrew and Christian scriptures are part of your heritage. These sacred writings are one of the many ways God speaks to us in our time. What is your memory of God talking to you through the scripture? Are there certain texts that have been a support to you throughout the years? Recall some of your favorite scripture passages and let them speak to you again.

Today I consider the holy days of my life. Sunday is the great Christian feast day, so today I walk through the Sundays of my life from childhood to the present. As a child Sundays linger in my memory as special. It was a wonderful day—a day to dress up, to celebrate the magnificent Christian belief that Jesus rose from the dead. I recall my childhood church where I received holy communion and celebrated the sacrament of reconciliation for the first time. I spend some time in my mind's eye remembering my early childhood faith and the faith of my parents. Going to church was a special part of Sunday, but there are other cherished memories.

There were special dinners, visits to grandparents or friends, homemade ice cream and special treats, visits to the lake. As I recall the Sundays of long ago I ask myself an important question. What has happened to God's command: Let there be rest? What has happened to Sunday in my life?

Is it becoming like any other day? Is it crowded with activity and busyness? Times have certainly changed with our fast-paced living, but somewhere inside me a memory of the wisdom of God's special request lingers. A part of me hears the call to restore the splendor of Sunday—to let it be holy again. On this day I ponder in my heart how I might choose one day each week to restore my spirit.

In this week of blessing it is also important for me to pause for reflection on the wondrous ways the word of God has moved through my life, molding me into the person I am today.

I have had moments filled with the sunlight of God's presence when a page of scripture suddenly became gloriously alive. New insights leapt from the word of God and I was filled with a deep yearning for life centered in Christ.

There are moments when I know in some profoundly new way that I am loved, that I am good, and that I'm called to be holy simply because one little word has entered my heart and spoken to me. I have memories of hearing the word read during eucharistic services and being mysteriously transformed. The word becomes flesh in me. There have been enriching times of sharing the word of God with friends, moments of truly breaking that word, like bread, and feeding one another.

What are my memories of being deeply touched and changed by the word of God in the scriptures or God's word to me at the table of daily life? I will live with these memories today. I will let the word of God in all its richness penetrate my being and mold me into the divine image.

Come Holy Spirit. Enkindle my life with a new fire. Let every word of God be like kindling helping to light this fire. Teach me more and more to treasure the truth that the word of God is active and alive in my life and has the power to transform me. Help me to remember your words from the past and to be open to the words you are speaking in this new age.

O Lord of the Sabbath, O Christ of Sunday, give us the wisdom to make this one day of the week holy for us and wholly for you. Slow us down. Teach us to rest and play, to celebrate, to pray, and to wonder on this special day that has been cherished by our fathers and mothers of long ago. Guide us in remembering the wonders of your actions in our lives. Amen.

Day 28

*If one part of your body is wounded
the wound is felt by all the parts.
If one part is blessed
the whole body benefits from that blessing.*

Read 1 Corinthians 12:12-30

> *Reach out and hold your hand. Put your head in your hands. Sit erect and use your eyes to gaze at something in the room. Now speak a word. Don't be shy. Any word will do. Listen to the sound of your voice. Stand tall. Dance a little. Reach down and touch your toes. Walk slowly around the room. Stand still and take a deep breath. Listen to your heart beat. Smell the aromas around you. Listen to the sounds. Hug yourself warmly. What a miracle you are. Just be grateful today that you have been made in the image and likeness of God and you are housed in a body that St. Paul has called a temple. Pray with your body today.*

On this day I will take a long, slow, reflective walk. As I pick up one foot and put it in front of the other, moving along at a comfortable pace, I marvel over the wonder of my body. This temple made of clay has served me well. What an incredible work of art each human person is! Being knit together in my mother's womb is an awesome work of love. How often I forget what a miracle of life I am. Gratefully I reflect on the perfection of my body. Everything works together for my good.

Is it not a daily miracle that my digestive process can turn ordinary food into nourishment, energizing me and giving me strength? I give special praise to my thyroid, that wonderful energy gland, a tiny power plant within me.

I sit quietly and experience my breath. My breathing puts oxygen into my blood. My blood flows through these wondrous vessels with proper distribution to all parts of my body. Another miracle!

The miracle continues as my brain, the first telegraph system, sends messages to the rest of my body. Truly the body is full of miracles. I sit. I walk. I run. I see. I hear. I touch. I smell. I taste. All miracles. And so I gently examine my conscience as to how well I take care of this sacred temple. Do I let it rest? Do I give it exercise? Am I conscious of the kind of food I eat? Am I aware of my breathing?

A further marvel is the tremendous resilience built into my body. How often it has been knit back together. I mend well. If any of these gifts have been taken away from me I still bless the Creator for this wonder of divine arrangement. Even in losing my health I am being taught. No longer do I take the miracle of my life for granted, and that, too, is a blessing.

Loving Creator, with divine attentiveness you have knit me together. With what deep wisdom you have designed the fragile, yet strong, beautiful work of art that I am. Today I am treasuring the gift of my body and all its wondrous functions. O Light of My Life, I cherish the loving way in which you have shaped me. Give me a deep reverence for the miracle that I am. Amen.

Day 29

Bathed in the soft light of God's glory,
your hidden self will come out of hiding.
So lift your power out of God's glory
that you may grow bright and strong.

Read Ephesians 3:14-15

> *For many days you have been praying with the blessings of*
> *your life. Holding those blessings in your mind and heart to*
> *strengthen you on your continuing journey through the field*
> *of your memories, we return again to some of your life's con-*
> *flicts. Today I am asking you to focus, in particular, on*
> *resentments. Resentments can be like millstones around your*
> *neck, weighing you down. They are not helpful companions*
> *on your life's journey. Try to be aware of, yet gracious to,*
> *your resentments this day. Talk with them and discover the*
> *underlying reason they linger on your path.*

I move now from the blessing of life back to the bite of life. The consoling part of the bite is that often it is this very sting of suffering that, when contemplated, understood, and embraced, can help my hidden self to grow strong. My life is so much richer for all the things I've allowed myself to see on this journey. Today in my own style and at my own pace I make a list (on paper or in my mind) of painful memories that still linger in the back yards of my heart. I am especially concerned with memories of resentment that I may be harboring. I want to be in touch with any spark of unforgiveness that lingers in my life. Resentment is a troublesome sidekick. It is kind of like traveling with a boulder rolling along beside me. It begets a burdensome journey.

One by one I look at the resentments that stand before me, from my childhood to the present moment. I welcome them into my life as I would welcome a troubled child. I spend time with each one. If one should stand out as a problem child in my life, I spend more time with it encouraging it to loosen its grasp of past hurts. I sit down in a beautiful spot and listen to its story. Resentments need to be understood. I try to understand the reason it stays in my life. Why have I chosen to keep it? This resentment enslaves me. It is a burden, slowing me down. Today as I hang it on the banner of my cross, I feel comforted. It has been an important teacher. It has taught me much about myself.

Jesus, these resentments in my life have controlled me for far too long. As I let go of resentment I can feel my hidden self growing stronger. I am filled with the brightness of your glory. And so I look upon the people I have resented. I send them love. I know that these people's lives, also, are filled with pain and burdensome things. I pray for them as I claim your healing. All praise to you whose power in my life can do infinitely more than I could ever hope for or imagine. Amen.

Day 30

Across the waters of life
I am walking beside you.
So fill your heart with courage,
there is no need to live in fear.

Read Matthew 14:23-33

> *Try to envision Jesus walking across the waters of life beside you. He is intent on keeping you from sinking into despondency as you recall broken relationships from the past. This day is for praying with the lost loves of your life. The end of a relationship can, at times, be as wrenching as death. Throughout this day, then, listen to the voice of Jesus assuring you that he is at your side. "Take courage. My relationship with you will have no end."*

How deeply I need to hear the voice of Jesus saying to me, "Courage. Do not be afraid," as I pray with the lost loves of my life. Each loss is a kind of death. Perhaps a relationship has been severed through divorce. The emotional pain of this separation lingers on. Memories are, at times, so painful that I tuck them away deep inside for a later day. I try to hide the scars of that broken relationship. I may do this through over-involvement, hoping to smother my feelings in lots of activities. Or, I may withdraw into an unhealthy silence, keeping the hurt inside. This divorce may be my own or it may be that of a close friend or a family member. Whatever the situation, I experience the painful severance of a whole network of relationships.

Perhaps my painful memory is not a divorce but the ending of a relationship that I had begun to depend on and treasure. That, too, is a kind of divorce. My human heart was made to connect, but suddenly something is not connecting. Life events change. New people enter into our lives. Misunderstandings occur. Irresponsibility happens. Distrust abounds. We let each other down. There is betrayal. We fail to communicate. There is sin. It all becomes an unhappy story. Perhaps it is so close to me that it becomes *my* unhappy story. Today, if necessary, I allow myself to feel the pain as I pray with the lost loves in my life.

O Jesus, keeper of all lost things, walk across these impossible waters with me. I offer you today my lost loves. There are people I once treasured with whom I have suffered the pain of separation. Gather up a few redeeming moments of these loves of mine and save them for all eternity when we will be united again in an embrace which will never end. On that day we will betray each other no more. Forgive us for all the pain we've inflicted on each other in our blindness and immaturity. Instill in me the wisdom to go on with my life and not to cling to my lost loves. Amen.

Day 31

Again and again I tell my heart
God's hospitality has not ended.
Every morning, a new beginning
with the sunrise, a new hope.

Read Lamentations 3:21-23

> *In your prayer allow those moments of seeming failure to visit you so that you may give them rest. May they rest in peace. May you also rest in peace. As you spend this day companioning your failures, you may be surprised to discover that they have been your best teachers.*

How strong is the desire in me to be someone! To succeed! To win! To excel! To be successful! How often in my life I've felt like a failure! Today I choose to be with that part of myself that has experienced imaginary or real failure. Feelings of failure can terrify me and rob me of hope. There are two kinds of failure I will pray with today. The first is the failure that comes from human limitation. If the truth be known, it is not really failure, but it feels like failure. I set my goals too high. I compete. I compare myself with others. Often I end up feeling disappointed in myself because I can't measure up to my own expectations or the expectations of others. I walk through the pages of my mind trying to get in touch with any feelings of failure that continue to sap my life of its power.

The second kind of failure that I reflect on is the failure that comes from sin. I fail to measure up to the deep-down goodness of my life. I settle for less than I could be. I wallow in resentments. I hold grudges. I cling to unhealthy ways of living. I live according to my own plan instead of God's plan. I often embrace violence instead of peace, selfishness instead of love, despair instead of hope. Sin walks through my life like an accepted guest.

This is the failure I must find the courage to confront. Today I sit in the shade of God's wings embracing my failures, my sin. Only with acceptance of myself and God's mercy will I be able to move on with new heart and new hope.

Loving God, I claim these truths as my reason to have hope. Your kindness and forgiveness are unending. Your compassion is constant. Every morning they are waiting for me. Your faithfulness is enduring. I embrace the reality of your immense love as my heart grows wings and I fly unimpeded to the mountain of your mercy. Amen.

Day 32

Be vigilant about the kind of life you lead,
you are to be wise and not foolish.
This age may appear to be lost,
but your lives should redeem it.

Read Ephesians 5:1-20

> *For the next two days we will be reflecting on the memory*
> *of addictions in your life, present or past, your own and*
> *those of others. Let this be an open and loving evaluation.*
> *You are on this journey because you want to be your best self.*
> *You want to heal. You long to become as whole as is possible*
> *on this path of life. With love, cradle your memories and*
> *give them a home.*

As I reflect today on my addictions, memories of addictive behavior in my life and in the lives of those with whom my life has been entwined come to mind. In the quiet of this moment I receive these memories. I don't fight them or judge them. I'm just with them. Being present to these memories can transform them into prayer.

My life is a well—rich and deep. It yearns to be connected with God. I am hungry because I am deep. With a bit of sadness I look at the unhealthy ways I've tried to feed this hunger. I begin with alcohol. It is easy to fool myself in this area. Because I am not drunk every evening does not mean I don't have a problem. I look carefully at my patterns. What do my memories tell me? When do I drink? Where do I drink? Why do I drink? I embrace any memories in connection with the misuse of alcohol in my life.

What about drugs—drugs of all kinds, including prescription medicines? Am I becoming dependent in unhealthy ways? What are my memories of peer pressure and the use of drugs? I do not judge my memories; I only feel them. I pray for the grace to understand my addictions and the courage to deal with them. If there are people who have caused considerable pain in my life due to addictions, I take out time to companion the memories that may return to me now. With as much compassion as possible I bring these memories to the chapel of my heart. I pray for all people who are chemically dependent. My heart feels their struggle deeply as I put them into the hands of God.

Jesus, in this difficult moment of looking at my addictions, I long to be rooted in you. You are my home and my hope. It is not easy for me to admit that I need help. As I look at the cross before me, filled with the bruises and blessings of my life, I ask that you stand beside me. Heal me of any denial on this journey. On this cross I place the great hole in my life and the lives of those I love—the hole that comes from being addicted to alcohol or drugs. Fill that hole with health, with honesty, wisdom, and courage. I want to live the kind of life that helps to redeem this age. Amen.

Day 33

Yahweh has this to say:
Put yourself on the ancient paths,
inquire about the way to life.
Where is the healing path?
Take it, and you will find peace.

Read Jeremiah 6:16-19

> *You are searching for the healing path. As you continue your*
> *meditation concerning addictions, try to remember that*
> *although they may temporarily prevent the goodness within*
> *us from revealing its face, they do not obliterate this good-*
> *ness. Behind the walls of our addictions our dear self waits*
> *to be set free. Today I am asking you to look more specifi-*
> *cally at patterns of denial in your life regarding addictions.*

Alcohol and drugs don't exhaust the possibility for addictions in my life. If I want to find peace I need to explore my addictions further. When I am addicted I am not in control. I need help. Often there is denial about my need for help. What are my memories of denial?

Am I addicted to my work? Am I unable to slow down and enjoy life, my family and friends? Am I willing to take an honest look at this addiction? Why do I work all the time? What am I trying to prove? Who am I trying to impress? Is there anything from which I am fleeing?

Am I addicted to sex or pleasure? There is a sexual energy in me that is powerful and can be used for good. It can also be abused. Instead of using my sexual energy to enhance my rela-tionships, it can be used to control, or I can use it solely for my own pleasure. I can become unhealthy in this area. This does not mean that I am a bad person. It means that I need help.

Perhaps my addiction is food. Do I have an eating disorder? Am I in need of discipline in the area of eating? Am I conscious of the kinds of food I eat? Do I ever fast? The real emptiness in me can never be filled with earthly foods, yet I keep trying to fill the sacred temple of my body with things that do not nurture me.

My addictions will never heal my loneliness; still I try to smother the ache in my heart in many ways. What are my addictions: alcohol, drugs, sex, food, work, smoking, TV, books, gambling, golf, prayer meetings? The only power my addictions have is the power to destroy relationships. They do that well.

Jesus, I plead with you who tried so hard to affirm and support human relationships, teach us to live in such a way that our lives will be drawn together rather than torn apart. Save us from our addictions. Save us from the evils that divide rather than unite us. Amen.

Day 34

No more lies.
Only truth!

Read Ephesians 4:25-26

Oh, we all lie a little. We lie most when we insist that we're right. Discovering truth is more important than being right. In our trying to be right we often put on a mask, and in some small way a mask is a lie. Today you are to pray with the lies in your life. Pray for the courage to see beyond and behind the mask. You are there— waiting to be found. There's no joy like finding your true self. Oh you'll probably lose your self again. But at least you'll have a self to lose—and that's what it's all about. Losing your self is finding yourself.

The time has come to confront the many masks of my life. My mask is not really me. It does not depict the true self created in God's image. Perhaps getting in touch with the masks of my life can free me of unnecessary burdens. I don't really want to hide behind a mask.

From my earliest years I have learned how to hide behind a mask for survival. My masks come in many shapes and colors. There is my *clown mask*. I wear it when I am afraid of my own depth. There is my *"I'm OK" mask* that I wear when I don't want anyone to see my vulnerability. There is my *stone face mask*. I wear it when I haven't spent time with my heart. There is my *mask of selfishness* that I wear when I can't remember who I am. There is my *"I'm too busy" mask* that I wear when I take myself so seriously that I think the whole world revolves around me, or when I've forgotten how to play. There is my *rattling on mask*. I wear it when I'm afraid of silence or as an attempt to impress by covering over my insecurities. I meditate on these and other masks that keep me from the freedom for which I yearn.

I try to get in touch with the memory of the many ways these masks have prevented me from living in truth. A mask is a great pain and a great lie. Yet as I pray with these false images of myself I will try to be gracious with each mask I discover. They cannot be ripped off in a day. Today I begin to keep company with them in my prayer. I pray before the mirror of myself with merciful eyes. I look straight through the mask to the free and simple soul waiting to be found.

Lover of Truth, Source of My Life, lead me back to the original stream of life where I was once created in your image. Fill me with the truth of that life. With gentle hands free me from the bondage that comes from the masks I wear to protect myself from the life for which I long. Help me to live with honesty and integrity. Unloosen the bonds of these masks. Let your own unmasked face shine on me. Bathe me in the true light of your presence. Guide me to the truth behind each of my masks. Encourage me to receive myself as I once was when I came forth from your hands: poor, uncluttered, and free—free to be me! Amen.

Day 35

Do not remember the sins from my past,
Instead, Remember me!

Read Psalm 25

> *Most of us have a few closets we've kept tightly locked, secrets*
> *we've kept from everyone—sometimes even from ourselves.*
> *Today take a look at the secrets of your heart. This retreat*
> *has taken you on a review of your life. I have wanted this to*
> *be a cleansing time for you—a healing journey. In asking*
> *you to look at your life's secrets I am not necessarily asking*
> *that you share these with another person, though if you find*
> *that helpful I would encourage you to consider that an*
> *option. If you feel called to seek out a counselor, I encourage*
> *you to do so. But I am mostly concerned that you are not*
> *hiding these secrets from yourself. What I'm asking, then, is*
> *that you unlock the closet and take a look around. Are there*
> *events in your life that you've stowed away and never really*
> *acknowledged as a page in your history? If so, use this day to*
> *pray with these secrets and honor them as part of the mosaic*
> *of your life. Even if you don't like them—they need your*
> *acceptance. They can awaken in you a deeper compassion*
> *for yourself and for others.*

God seems to have noticed my fears. I feel safely sheltered in the corners of the Infinite One's heart. Yet I cannot stay hidden forever. I have heard my name called and I must step forward and bring to God even the secrets of my heart. I reflect on things in life that, at times, I've hidden. I let the memories come. They quietly step out of hiding and stand at my side in trust. They have seen my gentleness and they aren't afraid of me any longer. They have come for my acceptance.

I explore the secrets of my heart—those things that perhaps I'm ashamed of and have never had the courage to face myself, or discuss with others. On this day I will finally befriend them. Guilt is useless. It does me little good. My heart is intent on understanding the shame and guilt buried for so long. I go all the way back to my childhood and memories suddenly reappear. They stand before me. They walk beside me. They trust me. I give each memory a name and a redeeming look of love. This is my life! I need not be ashamed. Under the eye of God I embrace the memories that I've pushed underground, the shame and guilt, the sins, the fears of my entire life. I reach out and touch them. I hold them to my heart as I would hold a frightened child. I accept them as part of the story of my life. I feel beautiful at last.

God of Forgiveness, it is good to discover that your eye is not so scary to be under after all. Nothing has ever been hidden from you. You know the whole of my life. In this new moment of shared secrets, I experience again your love and your mercy. I am so taken in by your infinite acceptance and forgiveness. You gaze lovingly in my direction and I am healed. Teach me how to give that same look of love to myself and to others. How wide is your embrace! Make my embrace as wide as yours. Amen.

Day 36

Pick up your mat and go home.
Take up your life and walk.
Welcome your life and start living.

Read John 5:1-15

> *You have probably known some discouraging days similar to the man in our scripture reading for today. There you are, broken to pieces with the disappointments of life, and everyone except you seems to find the healing pool. In your prayer today, go down to the healing pool. You'll do just fine. You mend well and you will find the waters soothing and medicinal. Pray with life's disappointments. Cast them into the cleansing waters and wait for healing. In asking you to keep company with life's disappointments, my intention is not for you to keep dragging up things you may have forgotten or repressed. Rather, it is one last opportunity for a review of life—another chance to pick up the pieces and go on with your life. This is your story. Every page is important.*

I begin this day in quiet reflection. I breathe in the disappointments that are part of my life's history. My breathing them in is a ritual of recognition. It signifies that I am not in denial. Then, as part of my prayer, I breathe out acceptance and healing. I want to be healed, so I go to the healing pool and wait. I invite my disappointments to sit with me at the pool. I speak to them, "You seem to be a part of my very soul and I ache with you, but life is bigger than this ache we share. I do not reject you, but you can control me no longer, for life is calling." I acknowledge each disappointment and name it that it may be integrated into my being.

The time has come for certain wounds to be bandaged that I may go on with my life. This is a "come-and-go" party. Memories may drop in for a moment; when embraced and accepted perhaps they will settle down in my life. If some disappointments hang around for a while, I'll spend extra time with them.

I allow the disappointments to come and go:

. . . parents who never spent time with me,
. . . a brother or sister I never had,
. . . a report card with never the right grades,
. . . a gift never received,
. . . a friendship that ended in rejection,
. . . inability to communicate with my parents,
. . . not fitting in with the crowd,
. . . not having the right home to invite friends into,
. . . having no one mature enough in my life to help me grow up,
. . . discovering I was gay and experiencing rejection by family and friends,
. . . discovering one of my children was gay and struggling with acceptance,
. . . a love never felt,
. . . a divorce or a death,
. . . never being chosen for the team,
. . . controlling or abusive people in my life,
. . . a sinful situation that I seemed unable to break away from,
. . . my many addictions,
. . . a job lost,
. . . a child I couldn't have.

(Since this list could go on and on, I suggest that you continue it in your journal.)

These life sorrows can sometimes last for a long, long time. And yet, these sorrows do not kill me. Life is bigger than my many wounds. Perhaps I have given a particular wound priority in my life to the extent that I cannot get on with living. If this is the case, now may be the time to go to the pool and claim my healing. Today may be the day to take up my life and walk again. Yes! I will take up my life and go on with living.

You, O God, you who are larger than life, you are my life! My life is in your hands. I am taking up my life today—the life you once lovingly breathed into me. I am taking up the gift of my life and walking on into the future. Fill every moment with new meanings. Help me to recognize the moments and be there—and be blessed.

Thank you for the bandages of healing you have used to cover my wounds. Thank you for the healing pools I never noticed until now—until now. Your faithful presence has awakened me to the beauty of my entire life—the wounds and the blessings. Amen.

Day 37

*Be still and know
that I am God!*

Read Psalm 46

The scripture text above is your assignment for today. This day is a kind of "time out." You are to decide how to use it and what the main focus for your reflection needs to be. Perhaps you will be led to do a brief review of your retreat thus far. You may want to spend your prayer time with your journal. Or you may be drawn to work with a specific area that has not been touched on in these meditations. You may feel called to simply walk through the day trying to be conscious of letting God be God in your life. "Be still and know that I am God," is a challenging call. (Pause here to make some simple plans for your day.)

At the End of the Day:

The dying and rising of Jesus and our participation in his death and resurrection form the heart of our Christian faith. In this paschal mystery we find salvation. During these days of retreat, you have been walking through your own personal paschal mystery, and in that walk, you have experienced salvation.

Tomorrow you will be moving into the last three days of your retreat. Having journeyed with the ups and downs of your life throughout these days, it seems appropriate for me to guide you toward a resurrection theme. The Easter triduum is a three-day observance of the paschal mystery. It begins at sunset on Holy Thursday with the celebration of the Lord's Supper and concludes on Easter Sunday at sunset. We celebrate Jesus crucified, buried, and risen. As we celebrate this tremendous gift of Christ's love for us, the past, present, and future become one.

Since these forty days have been a review of your life, I would like to treat the last three days as your personal Easter triduum. Whether you have made this retreat into a lenten experience or not, now at the end of your retreat I am asking you to pray these days as though they are, indeed, those three great days before your personal Easter—your resurrection from whatever deaths you have experienced on this pilgrimage through your life. Tomorrow morning you will begin with a meditation on the themes of Holy Thursday.

Jesus, in my heart there is an echo reverberating back to me in musical tones. . . . Be still and know that I am God! Be still, be still . . . and know, and know . . . that I am God, I am God. . . . I hold this echo in my heart as I stand on the edge of these three great days that are so central to my Christian life. The past, present, and future become one in this moment of now. Give me the grace of attentiveness and presence as I enter into your paschal mystery. Be my companion as I take up my life and walk toward Easter. Amen.

Day 38

As I have done, so you must do!

Read John 13:1-15

On this memorial of Holy Thursday contemplate how your life has been a eucharist: a song of thanksgiving. Two important rituals took place during the meal that Jesus shared with his disciples the night before he died. The first ritual was that of sharing a meal together during which bread was blessed, broken, and passed to one another to be eaten. The cup of wine became the cup of blessing because it, too, was shared. The second ritual was the loving action of Jesus washing the feet of his disciples. Because this meal was the last meal Jesus shared with his friends before he died, it is often referred to as the Last Supper. Jesus knew, of course, this wouldn't be the last supper. He knew that Christians throughout the ages would celebrate it again and again. He knew that the eucharist would be all-embracing—that his presence would be real and vibrant, far beyond the wafer we receive on Sunday mornings. Jesus knew that his presence would extend to the gathered assembly, his visible body on earth: the body of Christ. It has even been said that we should think seriously about receiving communion if we cannot receive every person gathered with us—and beyond.

Jesus knew that every time we gather around the table in love, he would be the silent, unseen guest, and eucharist would take place. He knew that the eucharist is all-embracing. It cannot exclude. Perhaps this is why Jesus didn't exclude Judas at the Last Supper. Jesus also knew that we would exclude some people from the eucharist, calling them unbelievers because not everyone believes in the same way. Consider these things today: What does it mean to be a believer? Are you a believer? How has your believing transformed your life? How well have you fed others? How well have you washed their feet? How well have you been eucharist? Ponder these questions in the silence of your heart.

I refresh my memory today. I call back into my mind and heart eucharistic moments throughout my life. Eucharist means *thanksgiving*. It often happens at a table, but not always. There is another table called *daily life*. There are many eucharistic moments right in the midst of daily life.

I envision myself gathered around the table with Jesus and his friends the night before he died. We are celebrating that great moment of thanksgiving for having been delivered out of slavery. We break the bread. We share the cup. We chant hymns. Jesus says that this is his body and we should do this often in memory of him. I recognize this moment as eucharist and I am full of joy that I can be present.

But something else happened at the table that night. I sometimes forget this other eucharistic moment. Jesus got up from the table and washed my feet. He washed everyone's feet, even Judas'. It has taken me a long time, but I'm finally beginning to read between the lines of that foot-washing moment. Jesus wasn't just trying to teach me by example that I should wash the feet of others. No, it was more than that. I'll never forget the look on his face when he washed my feet. His heart was overflowing with sorrow, love, and gratitude as he ministered to us. He had to wash our feet because he loved us. He was giving us eucharist again. It was as powerful as the moment he broke the bread and said, "This is my body!" As he tenderly held my feet he seemed to be saying again, "This is my body!"

Now that I've grown older, I look back at this moment and understand that he was calling us all to be servants—not doormats, but servants! The difference between being a doormat and a servant is the difference between living in slavery or freedom.

To be a servant means to let Jesus sing his song to us, in us, and through us. Only free people can be servants. Only free people can be eucharist for one another.

I am beginning to see how I sometimes allow my distracted and addictive life to smother the song of thanksgiving in me. I pause now and call to mind moments when I have forgotten to be eucharist—times when I've silenced the song within. Yes, there are days when my song has been unsung and people around me have starved for lack of eucharist. I forgive myself for these times as with great compassion I touch these memories.

On this holy day, I also call up the times when I have not forgotten. I can remember days when I've allowed Jesus to make music with my life—to sing songs through me. I remember times when I've handed out bread and washed feet with abandon. There have been seasons when I have celebrated the eucharist at the table of daily life as well as at the altar. I heard the echo of Jesus' words, "This is my body," and did not turn away. I have not always been inattentive.

Jesus, your words are clear. Your two rituals from the Last Supper live on in my life. Deep inside of me the call to be eucharist throbs unceasingly. I hear your voice, echoing through the ages, "This is my body!" "Yes," I say, as I reach for the bread at the altar. "Yes," I say, as I reach for the hand of my brother and sister.

Your second ritual, too, aches to be fulfilled in me. "As I have done, so you must do." Help me never to block your song of love in me. Lead me to those who long for their feet to be washed. And so today, my dearest Lord who washes feet, I sit down at the table with new confidence. It is never too late to be eucharist. Almost anything can happen when you share a meal. Anything can happen at the table of daily life. Amen.

Day 39

Into your hands I commend my spirit.

Read Psalm 31

> *The path you have walked during this retreat has, no doubt, at times seemed like Good Friday. It is never easy to look honestly at your life with an openness to change and transformation. Yet this is what you have done. You've told your story to God and to yourself during this retreat. You have been open. You've wanted healing. You've listened to your life. And in some way the cross has been your companion. You have tried to understand suffering. Stand beneath the cross of Jesus today and embrace the mystery of suffering— that mystery that none of us can fully understand. Touch anew the ways that suffering has been your teacher. I once heard someone say, "I'm in pain but I'm not suffering." At the time I wondered what she meant. Now I think I know. Perhaps it has something to do with acceptance. Ponder the difference between suffering and pain. Just be there with Jesus today and accept the healing that is within your reach. Hold gently the pain of the entire world this day.*

Today I'm contemplating the mystery of suffering. During this retreat I've looked at my entire life with an eye of acceptance. Now that I'm here at the foot of the cross what can I say that matters? I am putting my life on the cross with Jesus, but what does that really mean? I can't put any of these memories on the cross without putting myself on the cross with them. I cannot disconnect myself from my pain and suffering. And so I feel it all again: the resentments, the angers, the pain of rejection, the fears, the guilt, the sin and immaturity, my jealousies and envy, my addictions, and my loneliness! They are all here with me on this Good Friday. And now that I'm here with all this baggage I do not even pray to be rid of it. Standing before the cross I proclaim a gospel that God understands, "Here is my life. This is who I am. This is what I have to offer you. Here is my gospel—my bittersweet good news. I am wounded, broken, and scarred. Yet with all these burdens I am still able to be your song."

Even here at the foot of the cross my blessings seem to stand in the background. I invite them to come closer, and they do. They step forward. It feels like a great homecoming. Everyone is present. *Deep gratitude* is here. She stands close by, reminding me of all the ways she's blessed me. *Immense love* and *healing grace* are present. *Fierce yearning* is here. *Constant conversion* and *childlike trust* have arrived. *Always forgiving* is here. *Abundant joy* is present. *Lasting beauty* stands by my side. *Ever faithful* smiles through the crowd. Even *quiet peace* has arrived on the scene. The two sides stand and look at each other as if to say, "We're not really divided. We've always been one." The blessings embrace the bruises. The bite is gone in that embrace.

I look upon the cross and I am healed. I look upon what has bitten me and blessed me and I am mended. Yes! There is a *great mending* on this Friday that is good.

Jesus, never allow me to turn away from my life again. I put the gospel of my life into your hands. In your good time I know that you will wrap a cloak of transformation around me. Now it is time to wait and keep vigil with your love that has been poured out. In some small way I know that my love has mingled with yours. Together we will wait for resurrection. Amen.

Day 40

Mary of Magdala and Mary the mother of Jesus were watching and took note of where he was laid.

Read Mark 15:42-47

This is a day for laying things to rest. You have been on retreat for forty days. Imagine that you are in the tomb today. You are in the tomb waiting for resurrection. Strangely you are also outside the tomb. Thus you are able to keep vigil with yourself in the tomb. This is the heart of your meditation for today—keeping vigil. You sit beside the tomb and wait. You wait for life. You are keeping vigil with your life. You appear to be dead, but you are just resting. Look with compassion on yourself in the tomb and allow yourself to remember the forty-day pilgrimage you've just finished. Resting and waiting are immensely important for our spiritual growth, yet many of us abhor waiting. Resting is something we do only when we are so exhausted we can't go on any longer. Find a special place to spend part of this day. Try to be as quiet as possible. Rest and wait. Wait to see what signs of life may unexpectedly cross your path today. Put your anxiety aside and enter into the great rest.

The Great Silence is upon me. There are no words left. A quiet sadness fills my being. It isn't a sad sadness. It is a holy sadness, a peaceful sadness. It feels like I'm resting after a long, hard battle that I won. I am *waiting.* I am resting in the tomb. I am resting by the tomb. It is a Holy Saturday. This is the part of my journey to healing that I sometimes overlook. Its importance eludes me because it feels like wasting time. Nothing much is happening. It is called *waiting.* I am waiting today. I am waiting for life.

Quietly during this tomb time I pray with the Holy Saturdays of my life. What are my great moments of waiting? When have I been willing to wait for life to unfold? Am I able to wait or, in my impatience, am I one who pulls flower buds open before their time?

I must learn to wait. I cannot pry life out of the cocoon. I sit quietly by my tomb today and reflect on waiting. What are my memories of waiting for life?

Jesus, Light of My Life, now it is spring. Little buds packed with life wait for their moment of unpacking. Soon there will be a graceful, unhurried opening of petals. Small creatures about to be born are waiting for their moment of birth. In the nurturing darkness of the soil, seeds wait for an inner call to crack open and move upward and out into the sunlight. It is also spring in my heart and I, too, am learning to wait. I am waiting for the fruits of this retreat to be revealed to me. I am waiting for resurrection. The hurry in me is resting. I am keeping vigil at the tomb—your tomb, my tomb. Easter is very near.

Jesus, risen from the dead, anoint me. Help me to remember your rising so that I, too, can move through the obstacles that keep me from creative living. Heal this heart that so desperately hurries through life. Let the Great Silence unfold within me. Teach me to wait. If I wait long enough angels will come bringing news of that glorious new life called resurrection. O God of those who wait, send angels, send life. Amen.

Take Up Your Life
and Walk

There is a goodness, a Wisdom that arises,
sometimes gracefully, sometimes gently,
sometimes awkwardly, sometimes fiercely,
but it will arise to save us if we let it,
and it arises from *within us,*
like the force that drives green shoots
to break the winter ground,
it will arise and drive us
into a great blossoming like a pear tree,
into flowering, into fragrance, fruit and song,
into the wild winds dancing, sun shimmering
into the aliveness of it all,
into that part of ourselves
that can never be defiled, or destroyed,
but that comes back to life, time and time again,
that lives—always—that does not die.

—China Galland[9]

I have highlighted the goodness of life throughout these forty days. You have spent many hours honoring your memories. Your retreat is over; your life is not. As you begin again, take up your rekindled life and move into the beautiful ordinariness of daily living. The challenge now is to stay awake to the present moment, for this is where God lives.

You have been immersed in the liturgy of enhancing the quality of life. This was also the ministry of Jesus, who truly lived the present moment. He was unfailingly attentive to people who came for healing. He was absorbed in restoring and renewing the quality of people's lives. He did this by healing and affirming, teaching and feeding, by loving, living, and dying.

During this sacred journey, I have tried to lead you to reflect on the quality of life. You have meditated on the various ways we can become paralyzed through fears and addictions, and efforts to stay in control. We may be constantly trying to control life, rather than moving toward quality life. You know that sorrows not dealt with can cripple us emotionally and that we often lose our life while busily trying to make a living. You are aware that we are unable to take up our lives and walk joyfully and creatively into the future if we have chosen to remain locked in the victim role. Knowing all this does not automatically guarantee that our lives will be free from unhealthy living. We need to support one another in the ever present possibility of continued healing and growth. Sometimes we have to ask another person to lead us to the healing places, that we may be reawakened to the goodness of life.

In each of the synoptic gospels a story is told about some people bringing a paralytic to Jesus to be healed. After the healing takes place there is a quite firm mandate for the one healed to go back home—mat and all.

Matthew 9:6—"Stand up! Roll up your mat, and go home."
Mark 2:9—"Stand up, pick up your mat, and walk again."
Luke 5:24—"Take your mat with you, and return to your house."

I find it interesting that in each of these accounts Jesus asks the one healed to take the *mat* and return home. Putting yourself into this gospel story, I would like to suggest that after your forty days of healing, Jesus is also asking you to take your mat and go home. Don't just take off and leave your mat behind. The mat is an important symbol. It symbolizes all that pain in your life when you were living with your paralysis—the *mat* is all that stuff I asked you to look upon with compassion during your forty-day retreat. It has to go with you because it is part of your total experience. You probably learned a lot more than you realize while you were lying on that mat. You are not to look upon the mat with disdain and say, "I don't need this anymore." Although in one sense this is true. You don't need it anymore in its unredeemed form. But in another sense it is still a piece of your life-story; it needs to go with you. It won't be so difficult to carry now, for it has been redeemed through your honesty and God's healing grace. New resources are available to you. These are the result of the healing journey you just made. You are moving into life with a new attitude, with tools of hope and joy and forgiveness. Your compassion has been stirred, your love renewed. Your courage has grown. You have been awakened and your new call is to stay awake.

And so Jesus asks you to take up your new life and move forward. You are encouraged to be involved in the restoration of life. Get involved in restoring the quality of life in your homes and cities. Listen to people's life stories. Be a loving presence. Affirm and encourage. Notice the lonely. Sit beside the dying in their transition to another life. Don't just sit around hugging your new life. Experience it and live it to the full. Take up your life and walk!

How difficult it is to bring our real presence to every moment. How easy it is to take life for granted. We need reminders along the way: gentle nudgings and awakenings, sunsets and breathtaking panoramas, good literature and love songs, beauty and pain, death and birth. Yes, let us reach out for those gifts that will not allow us to sleepwalk through life. This piece of wisdom from Rachel Naomi Remen can serve as a daily reminder to each of us to stay awake:

> Life can become habit, something done without thinking. Living life in this way does not awaken us. Yet any of our daily habits can awaken us. All of life can become ritual. When it does, our experience of life changes radically and the ordinary becomes consecrated. Ritual doesn't make mystery happen. It helps us see and experience something which is already real. It does not create the sacred, it only describes what is there and has always been there, deeply hidden in the obvious.[10]

We miss the enrichment of life by not living in the moment. There are times, however, when God speaks to us so dramatically from the burning bush of the present moment that we cannot remain asleep. We are compelled into the mystery of "now." It is almost as though *the moment finds us.* One such moment was given to me recently and I was there to receive it.

It was morning. The sun was beginning to shine through the spaces between the leaves of the forest trees as I stood on the deck outside to greet the new day. Suddenly I was intensely aware that there was something unique about this moment. There was a sense of having been called from the house into the sunny shadows of the forest's green arms, precisely to be taught by life. I was in a beautiful setting for ten days of solitude, and although I had yearned greatly for this space and time, I was beginning to feel a tinge of loneliness as my restlessness set in. I was missing community and the comfort of sharing with others.

As I stood looking into the sacred forest I could see, through the branches, a glimmering of the lake off in the distance. Suddenly I was overwhelmed with an awareness that I was not alone. The clarity of that truth descended on me with vibrant energy. My whole being seemed to resonate with the song of the forest chanting, "You are not alone!" I was comforted with the realization that the entire forest was teeming with life. A whole community of little animals and birds of a vast variety, and all the water creatures that lived in the lake were there with me and were suddenly making their presence felt. Even the trees seemed to be chanting, "You are not alone."

Then, as if that good news weren't enough, a pileated woodpecker suddenly appeared to me. I use the term "appeared" because I had a strong sense that it was allowing me to see it and that its presence was a gift to me. These birds are rather guarded and only once before had I seen a pileated woodpecker so near. That was a number of years ago and that night I dreamt about it and it talked with me in my dream. Although I couldn't remember what it had said when I awoke, I had a tremendous sense of well-being. As I stood in awe of this new visit I remembered that dream and the same feeling of well-being returned to me.

This may sound overly dramatic to you, but what I am trying to illustrate by sharing this experience is that every moment is like this. Truly! Every moment offers a unique gift. If you are present to behold it, you could write a poignant story about each moment of your life.

The following episode, from a novel by John Gregory Brown, is a good example of someone embracing a moment so faithfully that a little story emerges out of the moment. In this story the painful circumstances that sometimes surround people's lives have drawn Cathy away from her husband. In being separated from him, she is also cut off from a young step-daughter whom she loves very much. Cathy continues to write her step-daughter letters even though she is not certain that Meredith is receiving them. In one of the letters she is describing the place where she is living—or, we might say, she is painting a picture with words. As you listen to this description you will know, without a doubt, that Cathy is living in the present.

> I'm in North Carolina, five states away from you, looking out across the pond to your Grandfather Reynolds'

old alfalfa and barley fields, which are now lying fallow. A nearly full moon and a hundred stars are in the pond tonight, and something is making the water ripple. The stars jump from one spot to the next, and the moon gets folded over and then straightened out again. Sometimes I think there's nothing so important as letting your heart wander out across a beautiful view.[11]

Every second is like this; each moment holds a story. The moment is never absent from us; we are the ones who are absent. Taking up your life is embracing the present moment. It is being open to the grace of every now so that no one ever need say of you what was said of a character in one of Walker Percy's novels, "He got all A's, but he flunked life!"

Of course, not all of our moments are so enchanting as communicating with birds or watching a hundred stars jump around in a pond. I was bitten by a tick not long ago and I became very sick with Rocky Mountain Spotted Fever. I was being called to take up my life. We might say I was bitten and blessed. The lessons I learned from the tick bite were, perhaps, just as important as the ones I learned on the morning when the pileated woodpecker appeared to me. In having to cancel the retreats that I was scheduled to lead, I was, indeed, being taught an important lesson. Suddenly you know, without a doubt, that events go on without you and that your life will continue just fine even if it takes a different route from that which you had planned. For me it took the route of some much needed rest. It gave me time to be grateful for life even in bittersweet moments. It taught me something that I already know but keep forgetting: I need to stop trying to control my days.

Whether we are living or dying, what counts is *being there*. Those who are dying often teach us about living in the present moment. In her lovely book *Refuge,* Terry Tempest Williams writes about her mother's dying. Her mother tells her that it doesn't really matter how much time is left. She says, "All we have is *now*." She explains that to keep hoping for life in the midst of letting go is to rob her of the moment she is in. Once again we are reminded of the preciousness of now.

On another day she says:

> . . . You learn to relinquish, you learn to be an open vessel and let life flow through you. It's not that I'm giving up. I am just going with it. It's as if I am moving into another channel of life that lets everything in. Suddenly there is no more fight.[12]

Death teaching about life! It happens every day. There is nothing like discovering you have a terminal illness to get you to appreciate life in all its ordinary moments. In sickness or in health, the challenge is to be awakened to the blessings at our side. If we've set up permanent residence in the past or the future, the pain and joy of the present can't bless us. Pain and joy are not always able to penetrate the armor of our indifference, our apathy, our inattentiveness, our distracted way of living. Though, at times, pain does a better job than joy. It is very difficult to sleep through pain. We are usually awakened. We may choose to pull on our armor again as we try to anesthetize ourselves from the pain, but the reality is that *we* have been *awakened*. The question is, "Will we choose, now, to remain awake?"

Throughout the gospels Jesus takes time to affirm life. He awakens us to the value of each person and the goodness of each moment. Let your soul fill up with silence. In the midst of the silence hear the echo of the voice of Jesus calling you to life. The following gospel texts are only a few examples of Jesus' passion for life:

- "I came so that they might have life and have it more abundantly" (John 10:10 NAB Rev.).

- "I am the way, and the truth, and the life" (John 14:6).

- "But now we must celebrate and rejoice, because your brother was dead and has come to life again" (Luke 15:32 NAB Rev.).

- "I am the resurrection and the life" (John 11:25).

- "My daughter has just died. Please come and lay your hand on her and she will come back to life" (Matthew 9:18).

- "Teacher, what must I do to inherit everlasting life?" (Luke 10:25).

- "Whoever follows me will not walk in darkness, but will have the light of life" (John 8:12 NAB Rev.).

- "One's life does not consist of possessions" (Luke 12:15 NAB Rev.).

- "For life is more than food . . ." (Luke 12:23 NAB Rev.).

- "Can any of you by worrying add a single hour to your span of life?" (Luke 12:25 NRSV).

- "What has come into being in him was life, and the life was the light of all people" (John 1:3-4 NRSV).

- "And just as Moses lifted up the serpent in the desert, so must the Son of Man be lifted up, so that everyone who believes in him may have eternal life" (John 3:14-15 NAB Rev.).

- "Yet you are unwilling to come to me to possess that life" (John 5:40).

- "I am the bread of life" (John 6:48).

If we want to live the abundant life Jesus came to bring, we need to practice living in the present moment. At the end of each day, why not glance back over your day to see whether you've been a good companion to the moments that have passed. What was the first thing you saw when you stepped out your door this morning? Do you remember? Does anything stand out as special from this day? What colors did you see? Were there any conflicts? If so, how did you handle them? What stories unfolded as you moved through the day? What did you have for lunch? Did you taste it? With whom did you eat lunch? Did the conversation enrich you? Name one piece of the conversation that you remember. What happened that gave you a sense of happiness today? What do you recall of beauty? Was there a little prayer in your day? How does it still resonate with you at this moment?

And finally, what did you touch today? Name one thing you remember touching. The way we pick things up, the way we touch and hold things in our hands, says much about our ability or inability to live in the present. Here we have Terry Tempest Williams describing the wonder of being present to an orange.

Peeling an orange is a good thing to do in the mountains. It slows you down.

You bite into the tart rind, pull it back with your teeth and let your fingers undress the citrus. Nothing else exists beyond or before this task. The naked fruit is in your hands waiting for sections to be separated. Halves. Quarters. And then the delicacy of breaking the orange down to its smallest smile.[13]

It's been a long time since I've peeled an orange with such reverence. Perhaps these are the little things we need to practice each day. It's the simple things that teach us best. When we miss those moments, we are missing life. Life enfolds us whether we receive it or not. The sadness is that when we are distracted, we can't receive life's blessing.

I truly believe that one of the most important things we can do for our well-being is to practice being present. So find an orange, an apple, a banana, a flower, a leaf, a blade of grass, a stone, or perhaps a cup of coffee. Hold it in your hand and receive the sacrament of its presence. Be there! Offer whatever you are touching the sacrament of your presence. This is not as foolish as it may seem. You are practicing being present. For those of us who live in a society that rewards us for hurrying and rushing, for doing more and more, the only way to learn how to be present is to consciously practice in little ways.

In Nicholas Evans' book *The Horse Whisperer,* a lovely incident is shared about the heart's longing to live in the sacredness

of the present moment. Frank and Tom are sitting by the camp-
fire with their father looking at the stars. It was such a moment
as one sometimes likes to hold on to, and Frank, the youngest
son, says, "If only you could make *now* last forever." They
remained silent gazing at the stars for a while, pondering Frank's
expression of yearning. After a time of silence the father replied:

> I guess that's all forever is. Just one long trail of *nows*.
> And I guess all you can do is try and live one *now* at a
> time without getting too worked up about the last *now*
> or the next *now*.[14]

Tom thought that was about as good a recipe for life as he
had ever heard. I heartily agree. Offer hospitality to each
moment and it will unfurl its gift of grace along your path in the
shape of a long trail of nows. That trail of *nows* turns into yes-
terday. It remains filled with stories you can connect with
through your memory—moments lost, moments found. It holds
secrets both lovely and lonely. Even the lonely *nows* become precious as we recall how we offered them hospitality and didn't
reject them.

Yes, life is a whole string of *nows* knit together with friendship and songs, heartaches and tears, fears and courage, passion
and compassion, depression and elation, patience and impatience, and more. . . . So don't miss life. Take up your life and
walk, whether it's happy or sad, angry or disappointing, ecstatic,
hopeful, heart wrenching or tender. You name it! Just don't miss
it. It is your gift to unwrap as you move through the hours. It is
God offering hospitality to you as you move into tomorrow.

Notes

1. Chellis Glendinning, *My Name Is Chellis & I'm in Recovery from Western Civilization* (Boston: Shambhala, 1994), p. 126.

2. Macrina Wiederkehr, *A Tree Full of Angels: Seeing the Holy in the Ordinary* (San Francisco: HarperSanFrancisco, 1995), p. 13.

3. Glendinning, p. 131.

4. Patricia McCarthy, *The Scent of Jasmine* (Collegeville, MN: The Liturgical Press, 1996), p. 55.

5. Demetrius Dumm, *Flowers in the Desert* (Mahwah, NJ: Paulist, 1987), p. 48.

6. Rumi, *The Essential Rumi*, trans. Coleman Barks (Edison, NJ: Castle Books, 1997), pp. 201-202.

7. Ted Loder, *Tracks in the Straw* (San Diego: Lura Media, 1985), pp. 14-15.

8. Robert Benson, *Between the Dreaming and the Coming True* (San Francisco: HarperSanFrancisco, 1996), p. 7.

9. China Galland. *The Bond Between Women* (New York: Riverhead Books, 1998) prologue, xv.

10. Rachel Naomi Remen, *Kitchen Table Wisdom* (New York: Riverhead Books, 1996), pp. 283-284.

11. John Gregory Brown, *Decorations in a Ruined Cemetery* (New York: Avon Books, 1995), p. 30.

12. Terry Tempest Williams, *Refuge* (New York: Vintage, 1992), p. 165.

13. Ibid, p. 100.

14. Nicholas Evans, *The Horse Whisperer* (New York: Delacorte, 1995), pp. 108-109.

Themes for the Forty-Day Retreat

Day 1 Your earthy beginnings

Day 2 Always known by God

Day 3 Conception

Day 4 Life in the womb

Day 5 Birth

Day 6 The gift that you are

Day 7 Dependence on others

Day 8 Tears

Day 9 The wisdom of the womb

Day 10 The importance of touch

Day 11 Hunger/unmet needs

Day 12 Awareness of beauty

Day 13 Classroom days

Day 14 Belonging

Day 15 Happiness of childhood

Day 16 Sexuality

Day 17 Growing pains

Day 18 Images of God

Day 19 Success and failure

Day 20 Relationship with the church

Day 21 Daily dying

Day 22 Death

Day 23 Blessings/virtues

Day 24 Baptismal moments

Day 25 Your potential to love

Day 26 The blessing of creation

Day 27 Sunday and the word of God

Day 28 The wonder of your body

Day 29 Resentments

Day 30 Broken relationships

Day 31 Failures as teachers

Day 32 Addictions

Day 33 Addictions

Day 34 The lies of your life

Day 35 Secrets in your life

Day 36 Disappointments

Day 37 Quiet day review

Day 38 Being eucharist

Day 39 Standing beneath the cross

Day 40 Waiting in the tomb